The Church and Abortion

The Church and Abortion

A Catholic Dissent

George Dennis O'Brien

ROWMAN & LITTLEFIELD PUBLISHERS, INC.
Lanham • Boulder • New York • Toronto • Plymouth, UK

Published by Rowman & Littlefield Publishers, Inc.
A wholly owned subsidiary of The Rowman & Littlefield Publishing Group, Inc.
4501 Forbes Boulevard, Suite 200, Lanham, Maryland 20706
http://www.rowmanlittlefield.com

Estover Road, Plymouth PL6 7PY, United Kingdom

British Library Cataloguing in Publication Information Available

Library of Congress Cataloging-in-Publication Data
O'Brien, Dennis, 1931–
The Church and abortion : a Catholic dissent / George Dennis O'Brien.
p. cm.
Includes bibliographical references and index.
ISBN 978-1-4422-0577-2 (cloth : alk. paper) — ISBN 978-1-4422-0579-6 (electronic)
1. Abortion—Government policy—United States. 2. Abortion—Religious aspects—United States. 3. Abortion—Moral and ethical aspects. I. Title.
HQ767.5.U5O27 2010
261.8'360973—dc22 2010012577

∞™ The paper used in this publication meets the minimum requirements of American National Standard for Information Sciences—Permanence of Paper for Printed Library Materials, ANSI/NISO Z39.48-1992.

Printed in the United States of America

To Archbishop Jean Jadot
(1909–2009)

[T]here is a whole generation of "Jadot-bishops" in the States who belong to the best. I wish that the Catholic Church in the United States may again receive apostolic delegates and bishops of the quality of Jean Jadot.

Hans Küng (on the occasion in 2005 of presenting the Hans Küng Award to Archbishop Jadot by the Association for the Rights of Catholics in the Church)

The one who voices his opposition to the general or particular rules of the community does not thereby reject its membership. Instead, he contributes to its growth.

Karol Wojtyla, *The Acting Person*

Reality is infinitely various when compared to the deductions of abstract thought, even those that are most cunning, and it will not tolerate rigid, hard-and-fast distinctions. Reality strives for diversification.

Fyodor Dostoyevsky, *The House of the Dead*

Contents

Preface

Writer

This is not a book that I have written with any pleasure. The argument is bound to offend partisans of both pro-life and pro-choice. Since I am writing as a Catholic about the official Church position on abortion, my criticism of pro-life arguments will be the most controversial. I am certain that many Catholic commentators will dismiss the effort out of hand. Opposition to abortion is so deeply entrenched as the Catholic position that any deviation, however slight, from official teaching seems akin to fundamental heresy—and that is my deepest concern: anti-abortion has become so dominantly *the* Catholic cause that it has quite obscured the deeper teaching of the Gospel. It is a Gospel of suffering and redemption that speaks as deeply to the anguish of having an abortion as it does to the heroism of the woman who defies the pain and risks of a troubled pregnancy.

I agree with the Catholic view that abortion is a serious moral issue; I even accept without qualification the official characterization of abortion as "an intrinsic evil." By no means should anyone seek a tranquil conscience about abortion. Nevertheless, I do not believe that abortion is inexcusable regardless of the circumstances of the woman who faces that decision. Public discourse has been greatly damaged by a conflict between those who seemingly see no great moral issue in abortion and those who see it as the overriding moral issue of our times. Abortion is a serious moral and social issue but it is not the sum of all evils. I have directed my criticism, therefore, to the statements of those church leaders who have been so flamboyantly condemnatory of abortion and the so-called culture of death.

Because I am critical of the absolutism of Catholic anti-abortion, my comments and conclusions are bound to offend many earnest people who march at Planned Parenthood, petition their congressmen, and are deeply and genuinely troubled by "abortion on demand." I happen to have good friends—laity, clergy, and hierarchy—who have been forthright in the anti-abortion efforts of the Church. I also number among the same range of Catholics those who are at some level disturbed by the harshness of anti-abortion rhetoric and the tendency of abortion to become the "single issue" for Catholics in the public square. I know from personal experience that not all bishops are comfortable with the stringent rhetoric used by their brothers in the episcopacy. In private conversation with some of these prelates, I have often found them warmly pastoral in their attitudes toward the tragic character of abortion. On issues beyond abortion, such as the perennial issue of contraception, my sense is that they disagree with the official position. Perhaps the saddest aspect of the current Catholic position on abortion is that, when some outspoken bishop describes the Democrats as "the party of death," no other bishop will stand forth and say straightforwardly that he is just downright wrong and probably a bit daft.

It is not only bishops who are silent. When I told a colleague at a prominent Catholic university what I was writing, he urged me to continue and commented that it was not the sort of book that an untenured faculty member could write. Indeed. There is a level of "irrationality" in the unbending condemnation of abortion that has created a silence in the Church akin to the silence of a dysfunctional family. Everyone knows that Father is drinking too much, but no one wants to say anything. To my lights, Catholics have been overindulging in hot rhetoric on abortion, but no one really wants to start a family quarrel. Personally, I would just as soon avoid confrontation on an issue that stirs such passion, but the Church's position on abortion has damaged politics, moral discourse, and the inner dialogue that should mark the community of Christ. Silence is not acceptable.

Ultimately, the retreat to silence is caused by the threat of Vatican condemnation for any deviation from the party line. One would like to think that even a modest review of church history would educate the Church about the dangers of rapid-fire condemnation. I dedicated a recent book to a mere sample of Catholic saints from Thomas Aquinas to John of the Cross and Joan of Arc who were at one time under suspicion, if not condemned to the fire. The whole Jesuit order was suppressed by Clement XIV in 1769. Only a slight lifting of the veil of placid orthodoxy reveals that the history of Christianity—and Catholicism is no exception—has been an arena of profound controversy. No wonder, since the central Truth is the deep mystery of God that, like the mystery of love itself in all its form, escapes even the best catechisms of faith or family.

Readers

Who should read this book? The obvious audience is Roman Catholics but, despite common opinion and official propaganda, they are a diverse lot running from ultra-traditionalists like *Opus Dei*, fixated on the Council of Trent (1545–1563), to reformers like Call to Action, who keep hoping that Vatican II (1962–1965) will actually be implemented. Depending on whether they lean back to Trent or forward to Vatican II realized, this or that collection of Catholics will suspect those who disagree of everything from lack of faith to heresy and sin. Given such discrepancy, this book concentrates on "official" Catholicism as that is expressed by Rome and the American Catholic bishops, the designated apostolic teachers of faith and morals. Should even a handful of bishops read the text and soften their anti-abortion talk and attack, it would have been worth writing. Nevertheless, I hope that all abortion opponents, Catholic and beyond, will read the book and consider how the arguments presented might change their attitudes toward the legal prohibition of abortion. Pro-choice advocates could also benefit by considering the negative moral and social consequences of "abortion on demand," the *de facto* situation into which various legal rulings have drifted since the initial ruling in *Roe v. Wade*. Sloganeering about "choice" can easily lead to trivializing the moral dimensions of abortion. Finally, I think that anyone interested and concerned about the political polarization driven by the abortion controversy should read this book.

This book is not in fact or intention a scholarly academic treatise. Much as I value such works and their discussions of the issue, any amelioration of the political dilemma of abortion will have to be solved in arguments stated in language accessible in the public square. No doubt this means a simplification of all the nooks and nuances of the reality of abortion in life and public policy. So be it. Nevertheless, since I believe that both pro-life and pro-choice combatants have vastly oversimplified the issue, my strategy has been to point to complexity even when I choose not to explore every variation in detail. I have included at the end a list of scholarly books on the issue as well as a chapter by chapter set of general references to statements and quotations in the text.

The Text

After chapter 1, which covers the dangers of the anti-abortion rhetoric, chapter 2 criticizes the anti-abortion campaign on the issue of law and public policy. I believe that this chapter offers a definitive check to anti-abortion politics. Staunch anti-abortionists will not be satisfied with arguments about the difficulties of anti-abortion legislation. They are convinced that the procedure is so heinous that some law or other should be enacted no matter how remote that possibility. There is no answer to such concern except to consider the moral status of abortion. Chapters 3 and 4 address morality and abortion. Because the anti-abortion cause is so simply stated—the killing of innocent persons—any counterargument will be more complex. The complexity stems in part from trying to clarify the notion of "person"—not an easy task. I have attempted to check any technical philosophic instinct so that the arguments are, I hope, reasonably clear. Nevertheless these chapters need careful reading. I cannot guarantee that they will break through the passions that propel the anti-abortion crusader, but I would be content if they give pause.

Chapter 5 may seem particularly specialized since it deals with the theological underpinnings of Catholic moral argument. This discussion is necessary since much of the anti-abortion crusade claims to rest on Christian moral principles. Whatever the limitations of strictly rational, secular rejection of abortion, one can claim that biblical revelation transcends all argument by stating God's direct command. I believe this is a serious misreading of the Bible and Christian witness. To the extent that I wish to address a *Christian* audience, this chapter is important. Should a secular reader bother with in-house theology and church culture? I think so. This theological discussion has larger resonance about how humans shape their history and final meaning.

Chapter 6 poses the following question: why, if the Catholic anti-abortion campaign falters at crucial points, has the official Church been insistent that anti-abortion is a "foundational issue"? Because I believe that reasons fail to account for the vehemence of the Church's anti-abortion stance, I suggest certain external factors in Catholic custom, practice, and theory that may distort argument. These factors in one way or another can propel the anti-abortion cause to the forefront of the official Catholic agenda.

In his commencement address at Notre Dame, President Obama called for "fair-minded words" in political debate. In the national controversy over abortion, neither pro-life nor pro-choice are exactly into "fair-minded words." Passions are engaged and rational discussion is often impossible. If this book does no more than temper *both* pro-life and pro-choice positions, I would be satisfied. If the reader only makes it through chapter 2 on the legal problems of anti-abortion, that would be enough. Politics isn't everything, but the damage which the abortion controversy has caused in the public square is immeasurable. The attempt to enact universal health care—a prime concern of the Catholic social agenda—has, at various times, been held hostage to whichever version of the proposed laws was the most stringently anti-abortion. All sorts of necessary legislation, from foreign aid to welfare, have been utterly stymied because of the poison pill of anti-abortion.

Chapter One

A Foundational Issue

The narrowing of the focus of religious engagement in politics to abortion, gay marriage, end-of-life questions, and a handful of other cultural issues is—it is a strong word, I know—a sin.

E. J. Dionne Jr.

E. J. Dionne Jr., political columnist and cradle Catholic, makes this accusation in his most recent book, *Souled Out: Reclaiming Faith & Politics After the Religious Right*. "Sin" is the right word, and the chief "sinners" in this book are those Catholic bishops who have been most outspoken in their opposition to abortion. There are other "hot button" issues for the bishops, like gay marriage, but it is abortion that has been in the public arena longest and stirs the greatest passions. Leading up to the 2008 presidential election a variety of Catholic bishops identified the Democratic Party and its standard-bearer, Barack Obama, as special threats to Christian faith and our national moral health.

> "The Democratic Party is the party of death." Archbishop Raymond Burke, former archbishop of St. Louis, current head of the Vatican's "Supreme Court."

> "I think that [voting for the Democratic Party] borders on scandal." Cardinal Sean P. O'Malley of Boston.

> "I think that there are legitimate reasons why one might vote for someone who is not where the Church is on abortion, but it would have to be a reason that you could confidently explain to Jesus and the victims of abortion when you meet them at Judgment." Archbishop Charles Chaput of Denver.

Bishop Robert Finn of Kansas City, Missouri, compared the choice in the election of 2008 to the world-changing seventeenth-century Battle of Lepanto, when Islamic forces threatened to overwhelm Christian Europe. He warned that Catholics who were attracted to Obama put their eternal salvation at risk. The statements of these bishops were not only severe, but they also clashed with the official publication, *Faithful Citizenship*, issued by the United States Conference of Catholic Bishops (USCCB). That statement attempted to place abortion as one of many important Catholic social teachings, such as opposition to the death penalty and the sin of racism. USCCB seemed to suggest that Catholics need not be "single issue" voters against abortion. Nevertheless, Bishop Joseph Martino of Scranton, Pennsylvania, broke up a parish meeting discussing *Faithful Citizenship*, and declared that there was only one issue—abortion. Whatever USCCB might say, he was the local bishop and his word was definitive in the diocese. Archbishop Chaput rejected the balancing act of USCCB when, in a critique of candidate Biden's "pro-choice" position, he stated, "Abortion is a foundational issue; it is not like housing policy. . . . It always involves the intentional killing of an innocent life, and it is always grievously wrong." For Chaput, all social goods are founded on the dignity of the human person. The fetus is a human person. As the most innocent and vulnerable of persons, the fetus is the most worthy of protection and hence the foundation on which moral concern for others rests. Denying the right to life of the fetal person undermines the rights of all other persons. It is hypocrisy to espouse high humanitarian aims like universal health care and ignore the "slaughter of the innocents."

Dire warnings did not stop after the election. American cardinal Francis Stafford, a major curial official in Rome, condemned the "deadly vision of human life," the "anti-life agenda" of the incoming Obama presidency. He compared the social effect of the new administration to "Jesus' agony in the Garden of Gethsemane." At the other end of the ecclesiastical hierarchy, the pastor of St. Joseph's Catholic Church in Modesto, California, cautioned his flock that anyone who had voted for Obama should go to confession before receiving communion. Though his bishop publicly disagreed with the pastor, the priest's position probably expressed the views of many of the bishops and pro-life Catholics in the pews.

The bishops in their official meeting after the election congratulated the president-elect, but stated in no uncertain terms that they would oppose any pro-choice moves on his part. The bishops' statements were often heated. "This body is totally opposed to any compromise," said one bishop. Another, "We are dealing with an absolute." This is "war" and the church should adopt a "prophetic" voice. They mounted a national public relations and postcard campaign in all the churches against a proposed Freedom of Choice Act (FOCA) that, they claimed, would remove all restrictions on abortion. (The fact that no FOCA bill was before Congress did not stay the campaign.)

Catholic spokesmen from pulpit to chancery office to the Vatican condemn abortion in an escalating series of characterizations: "homicide," "murder," and "genocide." No wonder it is a foundational issue. Strong words, but it is the contention of this book that such unsparing rhetoric is seriously mistaken. When launched into the political arena these claims mislead the faithful and do a disservice to the nation and the Church. Whatever the moral issues surrounding abortion—and they are serious—as *political* guidance these episcopal proclamations are sinful.

Several years ago I wrote a book titled *All the Essential* Half-*Truths about Higher Education.* I would be tempted to repeat the title: *All the Essential* Half-*Truths about Abortion.* By stating only a *half*-truth about abortion the bishops not only mislead the faithful at the ballot box, but they also fail to engage in any realistic manner the very issue with which they are concerned. There is a fundamental principle in all ethical argument: who wills the end must will the means. I would very much like to play the piano, but I don't practice. I do not really *will* the end of playing the piano; it is only a wish, a pleasant dream. Willing some end and not setting forth the means of accomplishing the end is a "half-truth." My desire to play the piano is a reasonably harmless fancy; willing some end that involves public policy while ignoring how to get there is serious business. Make the desired end serious enough and the failure to match ends and means is a disaster. The Bush administration may be admired for willing the end of Saddam Hussein's oppressive rule, but the failure to calculate the means for achieving that end resulted in a costly and as yet unresolved problem.

The bishops urge an end to abortion—they urge it with passion—but they have been either unable or unwilling to examine the means by which this end might be accomplished. Means have to be "realistic." I will not become a pianist by buying sheet music. If the aim is to prohibit or severely restrict abortions, what means would be truly effective? Failure to consider what really works has had many negative results, the least of which is that Catholics have been led on a fantasy crusade. Worse—the anti-abortion effort has caused a serious distortion of American political life. Worse yet—pushing abortion to the fore as *the* Catholic issue distorts the broader Catholic social agenda. Though the USCCB continues to promote concerns about war and peace, universal health insurance, and the like, the attention of the media and the extreme statements of prominent bishops inevitably lead to the conclusion that Archbishop Chaput is correct: abortion is the foundational issue. Worst of all—creating the impression that opposition to abortion is foundational distorts the Christian message.

Why Pick On Catholics?

Catholic spokesmen in the chancery office and at the parish level are not speaking to an empty chamber. The Catholic faithful have been energetic and insistent in protesting *Roe v. Wade*, picketing abortion clinics, and fostering local laws to limit access to abortion. While Catholics have been prominent in the pro-life movement, opposition to abortion is by no means confined to Catholics. Evangelical churches, the so-called Christian conservatives, have also been highly influential. The presidential election of 2008 would suggest that evangelical conservatives are even more firmly committed to voting against abortion than Catholics. Catholics supported Senator Obama, a presumed pro-choice candidate, by 54 percent, despite the dire warnings of their episcopal leaders. Whatever the voting pattern, the most pungent anti-abortion rhetoric during the campaign and afterward did not come from the evangelicals, but from Catholics. Although the arguments in this book apply to the Christian right, I focus on the Catholics for several reasons.

The Catholic Church remains the dominant Christian voice in the public square. The hierarchic structure of Catholicism clearly designates official spokesmen right on up to the one leader: the pope. While I know that some bishops reject the more extreme language of their fellow bishops, no one seems willing to publicly repudiate their statements. Given the Catholic governing structure, and the fact that Catholicism remains the largest single Christian denomination, the media sense the importance of the Catholic voice and vote. Reporters know where to go to get *the* Catholic view—or so it seems to them—and often turn to the bishop making the loudest pronouncement.

A second reason for focusing on the Catholic anti-abortion position is that it can call on an important and sophisticated philosophical tradition. Catholic opposition to abortion is more than a biblically based religious revelation, as it is with many evangelicals. Catholic "natural law" morality is based on rational considerations that cannot be summarily dismissed. "Natural law" morality is, however, a complicated tradition with many interpretations. Natural law ethics is often badly misstated by Catholic spokesmen up to and including the popes. Carefully considered, as it has been by Catholic philosophers, it is a position of great importance both in what moral philosophy can and cannot accomplish. In the case of the abortion controversy, the "cannot" is particularly important.

Last of all, I am a Catholic and so have a special concern over the failure of church leadership. I am encouraged to be critical of the bishops by the quotation from Karol Wojtyla, later Pope John Paul II, which is the frontispiece of this book: "The one who voices his opposition to the general and particular rules of the community does not reject its membership. Instead, he contributes to its growth." The quotation was made when he was Professor Wojtyla; it was not a maxim he was inclined to follow when he ascended to the papacy.

"Rome Has Spoken"

The adamant opposition to abortion expressed by the bishops already quoted was summed and reinforced by John Paul II in his condemnation of abortion as "a culture of death." The pope included within that characterization other presumed grave offenses against life: euthanasia, homosexuality, artificial birth control, and stem cell research. All these practices either deliberately took a life or prevented a life. The pope also condemned other deadly practices like war and the death penalty, but these strictures were often qualified by the complexity of particular circumstances as in the development of "just war" ethics. John Paul II's concerns have been continued in the writings of his successor and current pope, Benedict XVI.

To outside observers of the Catholic Church and to many within the Catholic community, the unanimity of the bishops on the abortion issue is only a reflection of its hierarchic structure. The pope appears to reign over the church like an absolute monarch whose word is law. That impression is certainly reinforced by the claim that the pope can speak infallibly on matters of faith and morals. If the pope says that abortion is always sinful, there is no room for argument from bishops on down to lay people like myself. The pope's sovereignty is structurally reinforced by the fact that all bishops, with a handful of exceptions, are appointed by the pope. Not only is his word law, but he is also able to assure that bishops will enforce that law.

The monarchic and infallible papacy is, however, in many ways a modern development. To take one example, for most of the history of the church, bishops were either elected by the priests of the local cathedral or appointed by the secular ruler. It was not until 1917 that official church law decreed that all bishops were to be appointed by the pope. Papal infallibility was a disputed issue up until it was officially declared by the first Vatican Council (1869–1870). Prior to that declaration, there was a strong and continuing claim that Church Councils were the supreme authority on matters of policy. The high point of "conciliarism" occurred at the crucial Council of Constance (1414–1418), which resolved the scandal of three rival popes. The Council clearly asserted its authority in a famous decree *Haec Sancta*:

> This holy synod of Constance, constituting a general council . . . does hereby ordain, ratify, decree and declare . . . that any person of whatever rank, or dignity, even a pope who contumaciously refuses to obey the mandates, statutes, ordinances and regulations enacted by this holy synod or any other general council . . . shall be subject to condign penalty and duly punished.

From the time of Constance to the first Vatican Council there was a continuing ideological struggle about authority: pope or council. It would seem that Vatican I settled the issue. Pius IX's comment, *Io sono la tradizione, io sono la Chiesa* ("I am the tradition, I am the Church"), seems to sum up the present situation of papal supremacy.

I cite this history not to argue for some other "political" structure of the church, whether conciliar democracy, the Orthodox patriarchate structure, or the various general synods and conferences of the different Protestant denominations. Fixating on this or that political structure can be a distraction in discussing the Church; the crucial issue is the spirit within which a structure operates. Recently, a joint committee of Roman Catholics and Orthodox theologians reached agreement on "the primacy of Peter" but, having said that, they remain up in the air about just what "primacy" should mean in practice. Presumably all Christian communities might agree on some sort of "primacy," if only because every organization tends to establish some sense of finality and direction. What seem unlikely to win allegiance from other churches are the monarchic assumptions that appear regnant in contemporary Catholicism.

I will have more to say about the problem of Church polity and infallibility when I discuss the distortions which a foundational anti-abortionism creates for the Church, but even at this point it is important to recognize that the long history suggests that papal instruction is not always final. Unless there is some opening for questions and dissent about "the culture of death," the arguments in this book will be dismissed as mere heresy. After all, Rome has spoken.

"A Decent Respect for the Opinions of Mankind"

When Thomas Jefferson penned a document for revolution, the Declaration of Independence, he thought that "a decent respect for the opinions of mankind" made it necessary to justify his radical cause. One of the most troubling aspects of Catholic anti-abortion rhetoric, whether John Paul II's "culture of death" or Archbishop Chaput's "murder without equivocation," is the apparent lack of respect for the contrary opinions of mankind—a class that includes many thoughtful Catholics. Reading the anti-abortion statements of the Church, one would have no idea that moral and decent people could possibly disagree.

Since the bishops claim that their pro-life stance is profoundly Christian, you would think that some attention might be paid to other Christian churches that beg to differ on the blanket condemnation of abortion. The American Baptist Churches USA, Episcopal Church, Evangelical Lutheran Church of America, the Presbyterian Church (USA), and United Church of Christ allow abortion under certain conditions. It hardly seems Christian to utterly ignore the considered view of those who disagree, particularly other Christian communities. If it were as clear as the bishops claim that abortion is "murdering babies," the only conclusion one could possibly draw is that these other Christian voices are incredibly stupid, delusional, or demonic. The existence of other Christian voices should temper the high dogmatic surety expressed in Catholic pro-life propaganda. Many moral issues, abortion included, require a balanced practical wisdom that simple condemnation obscures. When it comes to the political arena, the uncompromising character of pro-life accusation destroys the possibility of civil discourse. Anyone in opposition is in league with death and the devil. The present governing party in the United States becomes the "party of death."

The Religion of Anti-Abortion

Beyond political damage caused by the virulence of Catholic condemnation of abortion, I am even more concerned with how anti-abortion distorts Catholic Christianity. The current absolutist position is a threat to faith. The lesser threat: if you put forward bad arguments about such a vexing issue as abortion, people may come to suspect all your arguments. There are many positions taken by the Catholic Church that are of great validity—even some of the views on abortion—but pressing the position on abortion in overwrought rhetoric obscures other pressing moral and political concerns.

More damaging is that pushing abortion forward as foundational is a serious distortion of the Christian story. I devote all of chapter 4 to discussing how the abortion campaign has distorted the Church. I consider the treatment of the Church essential to whatever possible effect this book may have with a Catholic audience. I cheerfully confess that I am a "liberal" Catholic. To "conservative" Catholics this means a "cafeteria Catholic" who picks and chooses dogma and direction from the Church menu according to whim or the latest opinion in the *New York Times*. Obviously I reject such an interpretation of my Catholic bona fides. In chapter 4 I sketch out a theology of the Church, a doctrine of Creation, and a Christology. These are themes that I developed at length in an earlier book, *Finding the Voice of the Church*, published by the University of Notre Dame Press.

Publishing with the Notre Dame Press is hardly an official *imprimatur* for the theology contained in that work or the present effort. Conservative Catholics are free to critique my theology, but I think it important to point out that I have a theology. I am not raking through the catechism looking for attractive items. I gave a copy of *Finding the Voice of the Church* to my physician, who runs the local Natural Family Planning program for the Church. That would suggest a "conservative" take on Catholicism. When we discussed the book later, I was most pleased when he expressed surprise: "I sort of knew you were 'liberal' so I expected a watered-down version of faith. Instead you seem deeply involved in real issues of Christianity." I hope so.

My deepest concern, then, is in the damage that anti-abortion causes to the Christian story. Christian faith has its own way of approaching pregnancy and beginning life, but a genuinely Christian assessment of abortion rests on much different spiritual assumptions than the bishops' pro-life rhetoric would suggest. Promoting anti-abortion as foundational obscures the message of the Gospel. One hears more embryology than Christology. There is an important story of moral action and responsibility, there is a necessary story of crime and punishment, and there is an ultimate life story of sin and salvation. These stories are not the same and it is the last which is the Christian story. Pressing the *moral* story of abortion to the fore as the Christian story subtly but profoundly misses the truth of God's love and compassion. The amount of time, energy, press inches, and heated rhetoric spent on pro-life by Church officials skews the Christian story away from its central meaning.

Having suggested that there is a fault line in the Catholic bishop's position, I want to be an equal opportunity critic, and note a fault line in the "pro-choice" position. Pro-choice has its own firm grasp on a half-truth. Forced choice reduces the moral worth of an action. Defending choice is an important truth, but it is only a half-truth. The ultimate issue for morality is not choosing, but *what* choice. George W. Bush boasted that he was the decider; the problem with his administration was not *that* he decided but *what* he decided. The issue of *what* choice is one that pro-choice advocates seldom raise. There are various reasons good and bad for this reticence, but it goes against our common moral judgments to regard choice as the sole issue to be addressed in any action or public policy. In the long run, pro-choice should discuss the moral issues involved in the abortion decision. There may be some reasons for seeking an abortion that are clearly immoral and might even be checked by legal restriction. The most obvious would seem to be abortion because the fetus is the wrong gender.

Poisoning the Wells

In 1936, August Cardinal Hlond, primate of Poland, issued a pastoral letter on "the Jewish question": "It is a fact that the Jews fight against the Catholic church, they are free thinkers, and constitute the vanguard of atheism, bolshevism and revolution. . . . [I]n the schools the Jewish youth is having an evil influence, from an ethical and religious point of view, on Catholic youth." The cardinal went on to urge Catholics to avoid Jewish shops. He concluded, however, "One should protect oneself against the influence of Jewish morals . . . but it is inadmissible to assault, hit or injure Jews. In a Jew you should also respect and love a human being and your neighbor." What was the cardinal's message? How would it be heard? One could pick up the message "love your neighbor," but it is clear that the message about Jewish immorality was more powerful. However the primate may have qualified his condemnation, his words gave a patina of legitimacy to a virulent anti-Jewish sentiment that was to reach its most horrifying reality on Polish soil at Oświęcim. The Germans could not pronounce the Polish name so they called it Auschwitz.

Cardinal Hlond did not support the Nazi extermination of the Jews: "It is inadmissable to assault, hit or injure Jews." Later he would protest the persecution of Jews and was eventually arrested by the Gestapo while in exile in France. The American bishops quoted above—or their colleagues who seem to give silent assent—do not intend violence against Democrats, Congress, or the president. The bishops who spoke out after the murder of Dr. George Tiller as he was about participate in Lutheran Sunday services condemned the violence. But Andrea Lafferty of the Traditional Values Coalition probably voiced the attitude of the bishops who have so adamantly condemned abortion. How could he go to Church on Sunday and "brutally murder babies on Monday"? Just how far is the claim that Catholics are "at war" with the administration and its culture of death supposed to lead us? What are we to make of such grave accusations: "party of death," "deathworks," "betrayal," "culture of death"? On their face, such accusations would seem to support extremists who have coalesced around a "hate Obama" cry, some of whom are stocking up on guns "just in case."

Whatever the legitimacy of Church opposition to abortion, historical precedent would suggest rhetorical caution lest one give a cover to forces of hatred and destruction lurking in shadows. In my judgment, Catholic anti-abortion has gone much too far and created grave risks, not only in the extreme cases of murder of providers and bombing of abortion clinics, but also in the poisoning of our national political discourse. The excessive rhetoric of anti-abortion has played directly into the demonization of political difference that seems to have become pervasive from radio talk shows to the halls of Congress. Extreme accusations from certain bishops have received no ameliorating or critical public statements from the moderates in their midst or from the United States Council of Catholic Bishops. The president of the USCCB, Cardinal Francis George, suggested that Notre Dame's offer of an honorary degree to President Obama was an "extreme embarrassment to the university." The issue was, of course, abortion. Some eighty or so bishops joined in condemnation of Notre Dame; all the other bishops were silent. The fact that the university honored the first African American president, and that Notre Dame's illustrious past president Theodore Hesburgh fought for years as chairman of the United States Civil Rights Commission so that we might see the day when a Barack Obama would rise to the highest office, was put aside because abortion is "foundational."

Despite the damage to American political life and discourse; despite general public acceptance of the decriminalization of abortion effected, however awkwardly, by *Roe*; despite widespread doubt that fetal life—particularly in the early stages—merits the same moral and legal protection as that of an infant; and despite the fact that several other Christian communions hold that abortion under some circumstances is permissible, Catholic leadership persists in placing abortion front and center in communication to the faithful and the nation. Given the range of serious issues and sins at hand—poverty, war, discrimination, and the death penalty— the anti-abortion campaign constitutes a distraction and danger in political life serious enough to be labeled "sin."

Chapter Two

Abortion and Law

This book does not offer a history of anti-abortion in the Catholic Church. Its principal concern is with the strength or weakness of present arguments put forward by official Catholic spokesmen. Nevertheless, anti-abortion has achieved such prominence in current Catholic pronouncements that a bit of history may offer some perspective on why it has attained its "foundational" position. While it is clear that abortion has been condemned broadly in the Christian tradition, the understanding of pregnancy and abortion has shifted in ways that have affected judgment. Neither St. Augustine nor St. Thomas Aquinas regarded early abortion as the equivalent of homicide. For Augustine the fault of abortion was contraceptive; for Aquinas it was an issue involving the time of ensoulment. Before ensoulment there was no human being, so no homicide. Misguided developments in science in the seventeenth century led to the notion that the male sperm was in fact a pre-formed human being feeding from the female ovum until it reached proper size for birth. That view obviously led to the notion that the human being already existent must be protected. While earlier popes like Innocent III and Gregory XIV held to the importance of quickening for assessing the status of abortion, from the rise of pre-formationism papal condemnation of abortion at any time has been consistent. Modern biology rejects spermatic pre-formation, but anti-abortion arguments repeat the personhood claim for the fertilized ovum. Chapter 4 will discuss the issues of ensoulment and "pre-formation" in detail as they affect the present assessment of abortion.

During most of the twentieth century, the laws of the various states expressed condemnation of abortion at any time. There were, however, repeated attempts by various interest groups to eliminate this legal prohibition. Such efforts met with only limited success and public opinion generally regarded abortion as unacceptable. Thus, the decision by the United States Supreme Court in *Roe v. Wade* (1973) that made access to abortion a privacy right protected by the Constitution came as a great shock. Catholic officials were immediately energized into condemnation of the Court decision both on substance and procedure. Why should nine unelected officials overturn what seemed a general moral consensus against permitting abortion?

Catholic opposition to abortion needs to be placed within the broader area of Catholic teaching on sexuality. Catholic morality in all areas of sexuality has traditionally been strict and severe. Almost any sexual conduct other than married intercourse open to procreation is regarded as a mortal sin. While other Christian communities in the twentieth century had come to regard the use of artificial contraceptives as permissible, the popes have been forthright in condemnation of their use. After the Anglican Lambeth Conference in 1930 approved use of contraceptives in limited circumstances, Pope Pius XI, in the encyclical *Casti Connubii,* was unequivocal in rejecting any change from what, he rightly noted, was long Christian tradition: "[A]ny use whatsoever of matrimony exercised in such a way that the act is deliberately frustrated in its natural power to generate life is an offense against the law of God and of nature, and those who indulge in such are branded with the guilt of a grave sin." Condemnation of contraception remains the official Catholic position. Pope Paul VI restated Church opposition in the encyclical *Humanae Vitae* (1968). Condemnation of contraception is an important background for understanding the escalation of anti-abortion to foundational status.

There are two reasons for looking at the anti-contraception background. Pius XI's statement relies on an ethic of "natural law" deeply ingrained in the Catholic moral thought. I will have much to say about "natural law" ethics in the succeeding chapters. The other reason is that Paul VI's *Humanae Vitae* has proven to be one of the most controversial papal statements ever issued. The Church had but recently concluded the second Vatican Council (1962–1965). The Council appeared to most observers as a revolutionary break with the enclosed fortress mentality of the Church from the time of the French Revolution, if not the Reformation. Vatican II seemed to promise a more positive view of the modern world, with accompanying change in those policies that isolated the Church in its unbending opposition to "modernism"—a favored term of abuse in papal teachings from the time of Pius IX in the mid-nineteenth century. Not the least of the expected changes was alteration of the steadfast opposition to contraception. Paul VI, who presided over the final sessions of Vatican II, had taken contraception off the agenda and referred it to a committee of bishops and lay people. It was widely known that the committee overwhelmingly recommended removing the ban on contraception. The pope's reiteration of the traditional position came as a great shock. It was met with immediate vocal opposition from many priests. A number of national bishops' councils sharply qualified their acceptance of *Humanae Vitae*. In the long run, contraception has come to be treated by most pastors as a matter of individual conscience, rather than absolute decree. Current surveys of Catholics indicate that the overwhelming majority reject the notion that contraception is a grave sin—or any kind of sin at all. Paul VI was so shocked by the negative reaction to *Humanae Vitae* that he never issued another encyclical in the remaining ten years of his papacy.

Given the reservations and downright rejection of the prohibition of contraception, one can conjecture that opposing abortion may have seemed a "line in the sand" for traditional teaching. If preventing conception is a "grave sin," destroying the fetus, the successful result of conception, is even worse. Abortion became a prime exemplar of the dangers of secular thinking and moral subjectivism. So it has been argued by the recent popes and bishops.

Prohibiting Abortion

Abortion would seem to be an activity that can be restrained by legal prohibition, as it was prior to the Supreme Court's ruling in *Roe v. Wade*. Catholic opposition to abortion has been centered, therefore, on reversal of *Roe*. Is this a feasible strategy in opposing abortion? As noted in the introduction, a fundamental rule of the practical life states that "to will the end is to will the means." Once you have determined the end to be achieved, there are two questions you have to answer. Do you *know* how to achieve that end? Are you *willing* to do what is required? Whether the goal is regime change in Iraq or playing the piano, it is a mere delusion unless you know a means for accomplishing that end, and are willing to carry it through. You know you have to practice to play the piano; unhappily, you are not willing to do it. In the Iraq case, either policymakers did not know what to do, or they were unwilling to commit the troops that the generals advised were necessary. A similar failure to match ends and means fatally infects the bishops' anti-abortion campaign. Insofar as the goal is to eliminate abortion, the bishops do not seem to know what to do and, to the extent that they may fancy a change in the law to prohibit abortion, it is difficult to believe that they would be willing to accept the consequences of their rhetoric.

Concentration on *Roe* places the anti-abortion campaign squarely in the realm of law. *Roe* does not assert that abortion is moral or immoral—it just makes abortion legal within certain restrictions. The basic pro-life argument is that the Court should have recognized that abortion was such a serious moral evil that it demands legal prohibition. Advocating a law to prevent immorality, even serious immorality, is not, however, always realistic or even morally worthy. Moral positions do not automatically demand legal action, nor are legal sanctions necessarily effective. There are puritanical states where every fault and failing to which human flesh is heir has been forbidden by law. Although there have been temptations in our national history past to legalize every one of the Ten Commandments down to the finest interpretations thereof, that is certainly not the current mood of the country.

An example of delegalizing a presumed serious moral issue is the lifting of restrictions on contraceptives. As noted, the Catholic Church regards the use of contraceptives as a mortal sin. At one time, laws in the various states seemed to echo this judgment. Sale and use of contraceptives were forbidden by many state laws until the Supreme Court in 1965 sheltered the activity under a constitutional "right of privacy," the legal doctrine used in *Roe* to permit abortion. The contraceptive ruling did not stir any noticeable protest even remotely similar to the controversy over abortion. There is now a general consensus that legal prohibition of contraceptive intercourse, an activity normally carried out in intimate circumstances, is improper not least because the means of enforcement (police breaking down the bedroom door) is morally obnoxious and worse than the fault, if it is a fault. The Catholic Church continues to consider the use of artificial contraceptives an intrinsic evil, but no bishop that I know of is campaigning to reinstitute anti-condom laws.

If some sins are too venial or too private to fall under the purview of law, laws to prohibit some activities may be necessary because of their social consequences. Nevertheless, such laws must be carefully drawn if they are to be effective and not lead to consequences worse than the prohibited behavior. I regard the use of drugs like heroin, cocaine, and even marijuana as seriously wrong even as a private choice. As a college dean during the rise of the drug culture among students in the 1960s, I could never detect that drug use in any way improved the behavior or personality of the young people in my charge. It certainly devastated their academic performance and wasted their parents' tuition payments. Having said that, I think that the current U.S. "war on drugs" has created a set of laws that are ineffective, counterproductive, and immoral.

The war on drugs has not come close to eliminating drug use. Prohibition of alcohol under the Eighteenth Amendment had the effect of criminalizing trade in liquor and, in the judgment of many, actually increased consumption. Legal prohibition of drugs has certainly led to widespread criminalization of drug traffic. I would not be surprised to discover that driving drugs underground has actually increased drug usage. Lacking public noncriminal restrictions on purchase means that anyone on any street corner can be a dealer. Underage students tell me it is easier to get drugs than a drink. Finally, there have been immoral consequences of current anti-drug laws. Communities have been devastated by drug crime; harsh and racially discriminatory prison sentences have been created for even minor use. Does the failure of the war on drugs mean that we should make drug use legal? Not necessarily, but the legal instruments for restraining distribution and the treatment of users need a dose of realism.

The same questions need to be raised about reversal of *Roe*. Would it be effective in eliminating abortion? Would it be counterproductive, making the problem worse? Would it entail serious immoral consequences? A reasonable assessment of the consequence of reversing *Roe* would conclude that the ultimate result would not eliminate legal abortions, could well make the social problem of abortion worse, and would certainly result in the immoral consequence of "back alley" abortions.

Reversing *Roe*

Reversing *Roe* as the crucial anti-abortion strategy is a fundamental distraction and delusion. Too many pro-life pickets seem to think that getting rid of *Roe* is equivalent to making abortion illegal. Reversing *Roe* is, however, relatively easy compared with what would follow. Any legal approach to abortion in the United States must take account of our federal system of government. In the United States, there are quite separate legal jurisdictions for the national government in Washington and the various states. Historically, abortion was not a matter of concern at the federal level—it was a matter for the states. The legal situation in most countries is quite different; the national government's decrees are "the law of the land." An act of the British Parliament is, with some restrictions, determinative. In the United States, the federal government has strictly limited authority in regard to state policy—specifically, in the area of criminal law where abortion was traditionally classified.

An illustrative example of dual jurisdiction: the various states are sharply divided over the use of the death penalty, the crimes that lead to the death penalty, and even the methods of execution. The Congress of the United States has no authority on this matter. Death penalty opponents seeking a *national* prohibition of the procedure must bypass the Congress and argue their position before the Supreme Court. Unlike the abortion issue, the death penalty appeal to the U.S. Constitution is relatively direct. The Eighth Amendment states that individuals convicted of criminal acts shall not be subject to "cruel and unusual punishment." Those who seek to ban the death penalty argue that the death penalty is essentially "cruel and unusual." The death penalty issue is particularly interesting because there has been a strong move within the Catholic Church to eliminate the death penalty from the criminal code. Several bishops have taken strong public stands opposing the use of the death penalty. It has become a part of the Catholic "seamless garment" argument that life should be protected from gestation to natural death. Should the Court eventually overrule the laws of the various states—something that various justices have indicated a desire to accomplish—the bishops would no doubt hail such judicial preemption.

Given the duality of federal and state jurisdiction, pro-choice advocates saw clearly that the simplest and most definitive way to make abortion legal on a national scale was through a constitutional strategy. Similarly, the only sure way to prohibit abortion nationally would be through a constitutional ban. There is the remote possibility that some future Supreme Court would rule that embryonic or fetal life should be granted full "person" status equivalent to that of a newborn. Even anti-*Roe* justices, however, might think such a ruling went well beyond the letter and intent of the Constitution. It is reasonable to assume from comments of present anti-*Roe* justices that they would favor turning the issue back to the states from which it was "improperly" taken by *Roe*. In sum: don't count on the Court to ban abortion.

Another way to accomplish a national prohibition would be an amendment to the U.S. Constitution. The proposed form of such an amendment would declare that from the moment of fertilization a protected legal person exists. Relying again on the moral principle that willing the end requires willing the means, it is difficult to think that amending the Constitution is a realistic means toward the goal of prohibiting abortion. Amending the U.S. Constitution is a complicated and unwieldy process requiring broad consent across the various states. Any current reading of public sentiment would lead to the conclusion that no amendment banning abortion could survive the amending process. A relevant case in point: in 2008 Colorado voters were asked to vote on Amendment 48 to the state constitution. The amendment declared, "the terms 'person' or 'persons' shall include any human being from the moment of fertilization." Governor Bill Ritter, an anti-abortion supporter, opposed the amendment: "I do believe that it would be bad policy, bad medicine and bad law. . . . It would be a legal nightmare." Voters agreed, rejecting the amendment by vote of 73 percent to 27 percent. If Colorado, which elected an anti-abortion governor, could muster only meager support for a "personhood" amendment, it seems clear that no similar U.S. constitutional amendment could attain the supermajority of states required for ratification. (It is worth noting that the head of the Catholic diocese of Denver, Colorado's capitol and major city, is the much quoted anti-abortion spokesman Archbishop Charles Chaput.)

Since amending the U.S. Constitution seems quite unlikely, reversing *Roe* would simply remand jurisdiction back to the several states. One can accurately forecast a wide range of laws across the states from the permissive to the prohibitive. California had a permissive law prior to *Roe* and would probably return to that statute. On current evidence, South Dakota would seek to ban abortions. Realistically, reversal of *Roe* would not eliminate or prohibit abortion within the territorial United States. Abortion might become like the good/bad old days when you went to Reno for a quick and easy divorce. Oregon could become the abortion and euthanasia capital of the country.

It might have been less divisive politically if abortion had moved toward legal permission through legislative debate in the states. One should not be deluded, however, into thinking that if abortion were once again before state legislatures, we would be in the same situation legally or socially as in 1973 when *Roe* was handed down. The fact that history cannot be simply reversed has been made by various justices in their opinions resisting the overturn of *Roe*. For more than thirty-five years women have assumed that legalized abortion was possible in the United States. Whether their decisions to have an abortion during that time were moral or wise, the deed was done legally. What would be the social dynamic if abortion were again prohibited? The one obvious consequence of banning abortion by whatever means would be that pro-choice would replace pro-life on the picket lines. Whatever banning abortion might accomplish morally, it would accomplish very little politically.

An Object All Sublime

Imagine, however, that public opinion changes and an amendment along the lines of Colorado's Amendment 48 becomes U.S. constitutional law. The problem at that point shifts directly to the legal penalty. Whether one violates the U.S. Constitution or the constitution of the state of Colorado, there are penalties for the infraction. What legal punishment would an anti-abortion advocate recommend? The answer to that question is far from obvious and the bishops have made no public comments about legal penalties.

I can't claim to have tried every source or queried every Church authority on just what legislation would be recommended in the event that abortion is legally prohibited. I was assured by a prominent religious journalist "in the know" that the bishops were on record against recriminalization of abortion. If so, they certainly seemed to have hidden that record, and one could hardly come to such a conclusion from the statements quoted earlier from prominent members of the hierarchy. I did receive some confirmation in a private conversation with a bishop who assured me that the Church was not for "criminalizing the woman." Answering a phone inquiry, Richard Doerflinger, associate director of the Secretariat for Pro-Life Activities at the USCCB, allowed that, though not official policy as such, elimination of criminal penalty for the woman was more or less the position of the bishops. The aim of the law should be the abortionist who is "making a business" out of the procedure. The supposition that the bishops are not in favor of criminalizing the woman is significant—or it would be if there were a specific public statement to that effect from the USCCB.

Lacking comment about specific legal action, the bishops' arguments remain at the level of moral pronouncement with no guidance about public policy. My supposition is that most Catholic spokesmen would react as the readers of our diocesan newspaper did when I raised the question of specific legislation. Angry respondents countered that legal details were not relevant. One could not postpone the anti-abortion campaign while politicians(!) fussed with specifics. Raising such technicalities showed I did not understand the seriousness of the moral issue.

I do not believe that the question of criminal law can be evaded; specific laws raise further moral issues beyond the immorality of abortion itself. If, after reversing *Roe*, abortion were to be banned by any means nationally, or, more plausibly, locally in the states, legal penalties would have to be enacted against those who violated the law. What would be an appropriate and effective law? The ultimate "realism" of anti-abortion legislation hinges on the plausibility of solving the lord high executioner's "object all sublime": to make the punishment fit the crime. Failure to match crime and punishment undermines a law: too harsh a penalty and juries will not convict, too lenient and the crime disappears from public perception and the docket.

An instructive instance of the problems of legal penalty can be found in South Dakota's recent attempts to enact a restrictive abortion law. In 2006, the South Dakota legislature passed HB 1215, which banned abortions in all cases except a direct threat to the mother's life. Signed by the governor, on appeal the measure was put to referendum and narrowly defeated. The attempt to ban abortion was revived in 2008 as Initiative Measure 11, which repeated the language of HB 1215, but permitted abortion in cases of rape or incest. Initiative 11 was also defeated in the general election by a slightly larger margin than HB 1215. In the 2006 referendum, Catholics were urged to support HB 1215. The Diocese of Sioux Falls issued a special pamphlet to that effect. If one were to assume that HB 1215 or Initiative 11 constitutes a law acceptable to the Church, there is something radically wrong with the heavy rhetoric (homicide, murder, genocide) applied to abortion by outspoken clerics. The penalties do not fit the crime.

HB 1215 stated specifically, "Nothing in this Act may be construed to subject the pregnant mother upon whom any abortion is performed or attempted to any criminal conviction and penalty." Initiative 11 had slightly changed wording, but the same absence of criminal penalty for the woman. Criminal penalty was to be assessed only against the abortion provider. Providing an abortion was regarded as a Class 5 felony (HB 1215) or Class 4 felony (Initiative 11). A typical Class 5 penalty in some jurisdictions is the possession of two pounds of marijuana. In South Dakota the penalty for a Class 5 felony is five years imprisonment and a possible $10,000 fine. For a Class 4, ten years in prison and possible $20,000 fine. Five or ten years in jail would certainly make providing an abortion a high-risk activity, but it is not quite what murder, a Class 1 felony, would require. As for the fines, the FBI warning on your DVD specifies a maximum fine of $250,000 for illegal copying. Finally, it is difficult to see why there should be a possible prison term or a fine to the provider when the woman who presumably requested the abortion did not commit a crime. Assisting an individual in the commission of an act for which she is not criminally liable hardly seems like ground for criminal charges. It is not as if the abortionist coerced the woman into performing a criminal act from which she would therefore be excused.

Given that the South Dakota dioceses supported HB 1215 and Initiative 11, one might conclude that the opinion of the USCCB official was correct: the bishops do not aim to punish the woman, only the abortionist. The problem with stating this position as official USCCB policy—or Catholic policy overall—is that it appears totally incommensurate with the anti-abortion rhetoric, if not the underlying moral argument. If abortion is homicide or murder, it is impossible to see why the woman who solicits the abortion is absolved of all culpability. If she solicited the murder of her husband, she would be as guilty of murder as the one who pulled the trigger. Nor is the penalty for the abortionist commensurate with the anti-abortion claims. A fine or ten years in prison are significant penalties and would certainly check the abortion provider, but those are not penalties commensurate with intentional homicide.

In an article on criminal penalties for abortion, Richard Doerflinger attempted to counter these presumed discrepancies. Why no penalty for the woman? He points out that in the past when there were penalties for the woman and the abortionist, women were seldom prosecuted. The reason was that the woman was usually the only witness who could testify that an abortion had been performed. In order to obtain a criminal conviction of the abortionist, her testimony was crucial. The woman was given immunity from prosecution in exchange for her testimony. Over and above prosecutorial necessity, juries tended to be sympathetic to women, judging that, in one way or another, they were coerced into having an abortion. Doerflinger cited a study by James Burtchaell, *Rachel Weeping*, which argues that, all too frequently, the woman's choice is coerced by parents, partners, or her own anxieties. In our phone conversation, Doerflinger suggested that while the Church's goal is to prohibit abortions, one may need to compromise in the writing of specific laws. It would be an advance to establish laws that will diminish the number of abortions. Threatening the abortion provider would presumably have that effect.

There is something troubling about the strategy suggested by Doerflinger and what is presumably USCCB unstated policy. If abortion is really murder, as so many bishops aver, legal gradualism seems misplaced. It is true enough in health-care legislation that it is an advance to insure children or the elderly even if universal health care cannot be obtained. In the case of murder, gradualism does not work in the same fashion. One can expand the police force and change enforcement tactics to reduce the murder rate, but murder remains the same heinous crime whatever the reduction in homicides. Murder remains murder, a Class 1 felony, so that when detected it should be treated with the full force of law. Gradualism in the punishment of abortion is justifiable only if one withdraws the charge of murder.

As to the fact that under more stringent anti-abortion law women were seldom tried or the absence of criminal penalty in HB 1215, there are two considerations. First, there is strong evidence that the interest of older abortion prosecutions was not to prevent abortion as such, but to eliminate the dangerous practice of back alley abortions. Once abortion is carried forward by fully competent practitioners, this rationale disappears. On the removal of criminal penalty because women are often coerced into seeking an abortion, that argument can only be carried so far. Pro-choice advocates would argue strenuously that no woman should be coerced into having an abortion—or coerced into not having an abortion. Pro-choice's slogan of "reproductive rights" cuts both ways. What would the anti-abortion advocate say about the criminal liability of a woman who freely and deliberately chose to have an abortion? If abortion is murder, that would seem strictly analogous to hiring an assassin. Soliciting felony murder would make the woman as guilty, if not more guilty, than the one who pulls the gun or wields the scalpel. Finally, on arguing for *de facto* or *de lege* leniency on the basis of coercion, there are levels of coercion that may or may not offer excuse. Committing the deed because a gun is at my head is one thing—giving in to pressure from a sex partner is another.

In 2008 Bishop John Swain of Sioux Falls spoke about Initiative 11 in a homily noteworthy for its judicious and temperate tone. He said in the course of his remarks, "[I]t is not for me as bishop to speculate on legal theories or political strategies." There's the rub. Can one recommend pursuit of public policy to prevent or restrict abortion without some guidance about the legal specifics? Bishop Swain quoted from *Faithful Citizenship*, "[T]he process of framing legislation to protect life is subject to prudential judgment and 'the art of the possible.'" If the bishops are to be helpful moral guides, they should give some indication of what would constitute prudence in public policy.

Criminal Penalties Past

The South Dakota legal restrictions are, of course, only one example of an abortion law. Historically, common law did not restrict abortion performed before "quickening." Thus it was important in the South Dakota law to include the following: "'Unborn human being,' an individual living member of the species, *homo sapiens*, throughout the entire embryonic and fetal ages of the unborn child from fertilization to full gestation and childbirth." Fertilization was further specified: "'Fertilization,' that point in time when a male human sperm penetrates the *zona pellucida* of the female ovum."

A significant historical shift in the older common law understanding occurred in the British Crimes Against Persons Act of 1861, which was the official governing document until a parliamentary reform bill of 1967. The 1861 act covered abortions undertaken at any time, thus abrogating traditional common law permissiveness about abortion before quickening. For violations, the maximum penalty for abortion both for the woman and the provider was life imprisonment. No distinction was made for either maternal or fetal indications. Unsuccessful and successful abortions were equally punishable. Bishops who have characterized abortion as murder without equivocation should regard the Crimes Against Persons Act as commensurate with the crime. One can escalate abortion up to a Felony 1 classification with the attendant penalties normally attached to that offense. U.S. Senator Tom Coburn of Oklahoma, a pediatrician, at one time recommended the death penalty for abortionists.

While the Crimes Against Persons Act was about as severe as one could imagine, the history of its enforcement offers a different picture. Women were rarely prosecuted and, even then, the maximum penalty was seldom exacted. As with American anti-abortion prosecution, the principal target seems to have been the abortionist. Since the law made abortion illegal, only back alley abortionists were available. Again, the reason for pursuing abortion providers stemmed from the clear threat to the health of the mother and infant from these amateur abortionists. The authorities consciously or unconsciously seemed to downgrade the status of the fetus from the high standard implied in the act or expressed in the Colorado amendment. Women were not usually sentenced under the Crimes Against Persons Act since they were the only witness against the abortionist, and hence were given immunity for their testimony.

Change the conditions of the abortion, and the legal results change. One of the most famous abortion cases in British law was *Rex v. Bourne* (1939). Dr. Alex Bourne was a distinguished gynecologist. He performed an abortion on a girl of fourteen who had been gang-raped by multiple soldiers. Bourne turned himself over to the authorities, and was duly charged with a felony. The defense argued that the action was taken not only to preserve the life of the girl but also her mental health. Bourne was acquitted. The case is significant because it suggests that no matter how stringent the law, courts will not convict for compassionate reasons based on factors in the individual case. That the woman was underage, that she had been brutally raped, and the fact that the rapists were official guardians of the law probably entered into the deliberations of the jurors. The stature of the physician, his known competence, and compassion for a distraught patient removed entirely the interest in prosecuting dangerous back alley abortions.

Rex v. Bourne demonstrates the importance of circumstance in assessing the specifics of any abortion law. One of the reasons that even restrictive abortion laws such as the proposals in South Dakota's Initiative 11 permit abortion in cases of rape or incest is that the initiation of the pregnancy seems to be important in determining the culpability of abortion. Whether those exceptions are finally legitimate may depend on moral considerations that will be addressed in the next chapter; for now, I simply rely on a common moral assessment. Whatever the rationale, most people, like the jury in the case, would judge that it would have been wrong to convict either the rape victim or Dr. Bourne. A fundamental problem with drafting restrictive abortion law is the extent to which circumstances of exception can be written into the law. Circumstance cannot be totally excluded. In adjudicating ordinary cases of homicide, the law recognizes an extended range of culpability from intentional killing with malicious intent to killing in self-defense. This is straight murder; that is only manslaughter. Even when there is a loss of life, given certain circumstances, charges may be reduced from a felony to a misdemeanor to no penalty at all.

Are there circumstances that would permit legal abortion beyond saving the life of the mother? As noted, anti-abortion statutes frequently exempt rape and incest. Are there other circumstances not related to the initiation of pregnancy that would permit abortion? In *Bourne* the defense argued for the mental health of the woman. Should the mental health plea be allowed? To what extent should social or economic circumstances of the pregnant woman count in assessing the legitimacy of abortion? What about a woman imprisoned in wretched poverty with no personal or public support for a pregnancy? It would be immoral for her to kill a neighbor to steal his goods, but terminating a pregnancy so that she can eke out her own bare subsistence or that of her living children? It is not an easy case, and if the same question is raised, not in affluent America, but in the barrios of Latin America or the slums of Africa, the moral answer is even less obvious.

The variety, seriousness, and complexity of circumstances constitute some explanation for why "choice" plays such a large role in the debate about abortion. The situations we face in life and the choices available can be extraordinarily varied, complex, and tragic. Creating one grand general rule to cover complexity can seem daunting. Perhaps the best solution is to avoid rule and law and trust the moral sense of the woman. That seems to have been the intuition, however idealistic, of the majority opinion in *Roe*. Let it be her moral choice after consultation with her personal physician. The distinct danger in "leave it to choice" is the implication that the morality of abortion exists only in the eye of the beholder. "Choice" based on a thorough subjectivist morality need not be accepted. Subjective morality is both a general failure and insufficient to support the very pro-choice cause it seeks to defend. The failure of "subjective" morality and its implications for the abortion issue will be discussed in the next chapter.

Political Sin

In this chapter I have restricted the abortion issue to matters of *law* because it is in the area of law that the issue has been joined by pro-choice and pro-life combatants. I happen to agree with the Catholic bishops about the moral seriousness of abortion, but the Church's pro-life rhetoric projects a legal resolution to the moral issue that cannot be effected in the first place or made effective if actually enacted. Banning abortion in law is so unlikely that placing it as the foundational issue in politics is misleading to the point of sin. That is the point of E. J. Dionne's comment, which begins this book.

The Catholic bishops have placed themselves in a logical dilemma. If abortion is foundational—as serious as murder—then the law should be stringent for both the woman and the abortion provider. Senator Coburn's suggestion of the death penalty for the abortionist is on track. But the death penalty for abortion is not going to be enacted. (The bishops are generally against the death penalty in any case!) The chances of creating legal sanctions that even approximate the British Crimes Against Persons Act are nil. In short, no law is at all likely to be adopted that is commensurate with the hot anti-abortion rhetoric quoted in the introduction.

What about less stringent law? If laws such South Dakota's HB 1215 are acceptable to the bishops, it is then simply illogical to argue that abortion is a foundational issue so important that it demands voting against "the party of death." To make the foundational argument for anything like HB 1215, one would have to believe that an offense which carries the same penalty as possessing two pounds of pot outweighs national health care, opposition to preventive war, or unemployment benefits. In sum: if the rhetoric is strong enough to support the foundational claim, then no law can be enacted. If the law is as modest as the South Dakota proposal is acceptable, the rhetoric is excessive. Abortion cannot be the foundational political issue.

Simple realism suggests that even modest anti-abortion laws are unlikely to be enacted in the United States. If two conservative states like South Dakota and Colorado could not muster majorities for anti-abortion statutes, what are the chances in other states? There may be a few states, probably in the so-called Bible belt, that would pass anti-abortion laws in the absence of *Roe*, but even there it is unlikely that the laws would match the foundational rhetoric of the Catholic moral crusaders. The reason that even conservatives and prudent Catholic bishops pull back from highly punitive law stems from quite appropriate moral assessment that seldom strays into the anti-abortion rhetoric. I will examine these moral assessments in the next chapter, but before I do I want to point out one more reason why abortion should not be the trump card in politics.

The Catholic Church and the USCCB have an important agenda of pressing social and economic issues that should be addressed in law and public policy: peace, health care, elimination of poverty, ending the death penalty, opposition to racism, and so on. If one places abortion into this list of social concerns, abortion seems markedly different. No law will actually prevent women seeking and obtaining abortions. Everyone agrees that if abortion is illegal, illegal abortions will be performed. Many years ago Daniel Callahan undertook a worldwide survey of abortion laws and practices. He concluded that, no matter how stringent the law, women sought and obtained abortions.

The fact that law will not actually eliminate abortions should give pause to policymakers and the bishops because many of the other social goals can be completely and definitively effected by law. The death penalty can be abolished with the stroke of a pen. When Mario Cuomo was governor of New York, he simply vetoed every death penalty bill that came to his desk. There were no executions in New York, and no lynch mobs sprang up to practice "back alley executions." One either goes to war or one does not. Universal health care legislation may be difficult to draft and pass, but it is eminently the work of policy. It may be crass realism, but it makes sense to concentrate political attention on goals that can actually be attained by law and policy, rather than promoting laws that express a moral concern but fail in their practical effect.

The reason that abortion cannot be the most important issue facing policymakers is that while politicians enact policy, they do not, despite moral pronouncements during elections, effect morality when in office. Abortion prohibition means specific criminal codes that are either modest in their sanctions (incommensurate with the moral gravity alleged) or, if restrictive and punitive, significantly unenforceable. In contrast, several of the issues that seem to be of lesser seriousness in statements by the USCCB are eminently capable of *policy* resolution.

There Oughta Be a Law!

Abortion is a serious moral issue and the Church should do everything it can to reduce resort to abortion. The law can be one instrument in that effort, but legal prohibition is not only highly unlikely to occur, it also would not stop women from obtaining abortions—it would only drive the procedure underground. If prohibition is not a legal option, there are other legal ways to address the crises in the life of the woman that lead to abortion. Some legal strategies involve social programs that change the external conditions which often lead women to choose abortion. Others speak to prudent steps that an individual woman might be required to take in order to obtain an abortion.

Regarding social programs, the prudential course for the USCCB would be to give clear support to the so-called 95-10 package of legislative initiatives proposed by Democrats for Life, rather than a futile campaign to recriminalize abortion. While there has been some recognition of the value of the 95-10 proposals, the bishops have not been able to get around opposition to *Roe* as their main issue. The proposed Pregnant Women Support Act starts with establishing programs that prevent pregnancy in the first place. Abstinence is to be encouraged by public campaign while access to contraceptives is also regarded as necessary. When it comes to problem pregnancies, the legislation proposes a variety of measures from studies of why women seek abortions to an adoption tax credit to encourage women to carry the child and families to adopt. A toll-free number to receive information about assistance programs, maternity counseling, proper health support, and visiting nurse care are part of the overall agenda. It is projected that these measures would reduce the number of abortions by 95 percent in ten years. While one may doubt that the results would be as positive as the legislation forecasts, it is likely that it would reduce the number of abortions.

In terms of accessing abortion, the other legal possibility for reducing the number of abortions involves regulations that might govern a woman's access to legal abortion. America is unique in requiring such minimal review prior to abortion. In Britain one needs the concurring opinion of two physicians; in Germany there is required counseling before an abortion sign-off. Prior notification of the parents of underage women, spouses, or partners before obtaining an abortion has been suggested by some American states. Admittedly, there are many cases when such notification would be inappropriate and even dangerous for the woman. Attempts have been made to provide circumvention of notification when circumstances dictate, but these have not been upheld. There are two significant problems with setting any conditions that must be fulfilled prior to obtaining an abortion. The most direct and formidable is that *Roe* is a constitutional ruling. Given that access to abortion in the first trimester is regarded as a *constitutionally* protected right, the Court has determined, as it does with any constitutional right, that there can be no "undue burden" exacted by the Congress or the various states that would block that right *de facto*. There is a constitutional right to free speech and assembly. Authorities may, however, place certain reasonable restrictions on the exercise of this right, such as assuring that there is adequate safety and security at a public gathering. However, exacting an enormous fee for police protection would be an undue burden, which would effectively block the exercise of the right. The court properly strikes down such *de facto* restrictions.

In a series of rulings, the Court has struck down a variety of state-imposed conditions on access to abortion, such as parental notification, as undue burden. However, waiting periods and some required health counseling have been deemed reasonable without restricting the right. It is not possible to predict how the Court may rule on specific requirements, though there has been a tendency with the appointment of more "conservative" justices to be more permissive on restrictions that seem reasonable to protect the health of the woman, and to assure that her decision is a considered one. My personal view is that the Court has been too severe in striking down what seem to be reasonable restrictions.

Other than the personal views about abortion that may be held by individual justices, I think that the root cause of these stringent rulings is the placement of the issue under constitutional mandate. The strongest argument for returning jurisdiction of abortion back to the states is that one would not face the constitutional problem. When it comes to a basic *constitutional* right, it is understandable that one wants to eliminate even a shadow of undue burden. In less ponderous legislation regarding sound public policy, sensible restrictions are more likely to be admitted. On the other hand, anti-abortion advocates should not delude themselves into believing that "undue burden" concerns would not arise if the issue were back in the hands of state legislation. Any legislation from the Constitution on down will rule out *de facto* circumvention of the law's clear intent.

The other major obstacle to setting up a regime of sensible restrictions prior to the abortion decision is the steadfast opposition to all restrictions, no matter how seemingly innocuous, by various pro-choice advocacy groups like Pro Choice America and the National Organization of Women (NOW). I would conjecture that there are two reasons for this blanket opposition. Neither is very praiseworthy. The most dubious is the fear that if even the smallest restriction is permitted, it will create the famous "slippery slope" syndrome. If this restriction is OK, why not this other one, and how about that one? Pretty soon, while the right to obtain an abortion remains, it has been so stitched around with waiting periods, counseling, notification, and the like that women will be discouraged from getting involved in the mess of procedures. Getting an abortion will become like deciphering the IRS code. The fear of slipping down the slope to effective prohibition of abortion saddles pro-choice with the same unbending stance as the National Rifle Association's (NRA) opposition to any restriction on gun ownership. Since the Second Amendment of the U.S. Constitution presumably grants citizens the right to bear arms, the NRA argues that there is a constitutional right to own *any* weapon from hunting rifles to hand guns to "street sweeper" machine guns. Limit any weapon, and who knows how far the restrictions will go!

If one admits a right to gun ownership or to obtaining an abortion, there is no reason why one could not enact sensible restrictions, like licensing requirements on gun owners, or compulsory counseling about the consequences of or alternatives to abortion for women. The problem with no restriction is that it suggests that abortion is an indifferent procedure in which the life of the fetus is wholly discounted. It is like arguing that owning a deadly weapon is a matter of social indifference, so buy whatever you want.

A more fundamental reason for the pro-choice opposition to restrictions is a failure to deal with the moral dimensions of the abortion. I have already indicated in the introduction the apparent limitation of pro-choice advocacy as a moral position. While there is no moral content to a forced choice, the morality of an action is not based on the fact that it is chosen but on *what* is chosen. While it is understandable that pro-choice advocates want to release women from legal coercion, it is just not sufficient to leave the whole issue of abortion as a matter of choice. The temptation to fixate on choice alone is often based on a distinctly faulty theory: subjectivism, or a utilitarian "ends justify the means" morality. Neither of these theories offers an adequate account of morality. To the extent that pro-choice advocacy rests on these unstated moral theories, the argument legitimating abortion is without proper moral foundation. Pro-choice advocates would be well advised to deal with abortion in a clearly moral manner both in theory and full description. As I will suggest later, a sensible assessment of the morality of abortion may still legitimate "pro-choice" public policy.

In the long run, moral assessment of the complexities of abortion should determine the legal situation. In my opinion, neither pro-life nor pro-choice has a moral theory strong enough to support their respective positions. While I believe that this chapter should be sufficient to persuade the Catholic bishops to abandon their efforts to prohibit abortion in law because of the sheer futility of the cause, I am equally certain that they, like many pro-lifers, will not be at all convinced to do so. For them, abortion is such a heinous evil that legal prohibition must be pursued in whatever prophetic mode can be called forth. The Church may be a voice crying in the wilderness of a culture of death, but that is its task and destiny. While I am not hopeful that mere argument can pierce the passions of the pro-life and pro-choice campaigns, I want to offer in the next two chapters some comments on the moral dimensions of abortion, which, if they do not change minds, may cool talk and tempers.

Chapter Three

Morality: Not Too Much Theory

The previous chapter focused on how the anti-abortion campaign in stated policy and flamboyant rhetoric damages the body politic. A staunch anti-abortion critic will, however, dismiss all the technicalities of amending the Constitution, criminal law, or the behavior of juries and insist that abortion is, as Archbishop Chaput has put it, "murder without equivocation." Abortion is so seriously immoral that a legal prohibition must be sought no matter how difficult the process currently appears. As much as I believe the legal realities should be sufficient to dampen anti-abortion rhetoric, and as much as I am tempted to leave the moral issue aside, morality must be addressed because understanding the moral complexity of the issue should influence the law—though not as the official Catholic arguments would suggest.

In order to discuss the moral issues, I will have to touch on moral theory. I do so with apprehension. Ethics has been a major concern of the philosophic tradition from the time of Plato. It has produced works of great profundity, but also texts of exhausting technical intricacy. Even touching the margins of grand ethical theory is problematic and subject to qualification beyond end. I have subtitled this chapter "not too much theory." I intend the phrase in two senses. First, I want to reassure the reader that, as far as possible, the argument can be understood even if you have never taken Philosophy 101. Second, the title expresses the basic thesis of the chapter: too much theory can distort moral *deliberation*—which is the tough part of the moral life. Moral deliberation and decision are finally guided by what Aristotle called "practical wisdom." Practical wisdom is more art than theory—a product of experience, not direct rational deduction.

A more important motive for avoiding high philosophy is that whatever may be gained by argumentative elegance is likely to be lost in the political arena where the abortion issue most needs resolution. Even in moral theory, when arguments lead too far beyond common experience, a heavy burden of proof lies with the theory. The moral assessment of most Catholics is that artificial contraception is not immoral; the burden of proof is on Catholic authorities to prove otherwise. So far their arguments are based on theories that, whatever their value, seem too abstract when applied to actual life. Abstract theory is not exclusive to pro-life; it is a fault line across the pro-life/pro-choice divide. The abstraction of abortion polemics may account for why various national polls show a majority are pro-choice *and* anti-abortion. Common opinion may be more sensible than the ideological war.

Abortion Is a Moral Issue

Is abortion a moral problem? There is no point writing a chapter on morality if it is not. It is hard to imagine that pregnancy does not present a host of moral concerns. One need not accept the premise of pro-life that we are dealing with a full-fledged "person" from the moment of conception to hold that the fetus has moral standing and should not be casually discounted. We have, after all, extended moral protection to the planet's various endangered species. We would morally condemn someone who put down the family dog simply out of dislike for the poor mutt. It would certainly seem, then, that there is a *prima facie* case for treating the human fetus with care. It takes considerable ideological fascination to think that nascent life does not have inherent worth. Women who rejoice in a pregnancy or mourn a miscarriage are not deluded. Something of great value is involved.

The problem with the moral standing of the fetus is how great is that standing. Does moral standing vary with the stages of development? (I shall use the term "fetus" throughout as shorthand for all stages of development from the "conceptus" onward.) The strong pro-lifer argues for full moral standing equivalent to a newborn from the moment of conception. The moderate pro-life or pro-choice advocate sees evolving levels of moral standing intersecting in various ways with other moral considerations impinging on the pregnant woman. The ultra-pro-choice position diminishes the moral standing of the fetus—at least in the early stages—to zero, so that any choice, however inconsequential, is morally legitimate—rather like the choice for cosmetic plastic surgery. But even cosmetic surgery raises moral issues, however offending the nose in question. Later I will attempt to disentangle the notion of "person" that is the central value term in the argument, but, for now, it seems eminently reasonable to assume that abortion, in one way or another, requires moral assessment.

For Catholics abortion is not only a moral issue, but it is also so serious that it has been labeled as foundational, more serious than the range of other issues that are part of the Church's social agenda. If abortion is such a grave matter, it seems obvious that it demands legal restriction. But, as pointed out earlier, serious immorality and legal restriction are not necessarily connected. None of the traditional seven deadly sins—lust, gluttony, greed, sloth, wrath, envy, and pride—are likely to be punished in law. These sins are matters of character that may lead to criminal behavior, but usually only produce quite distressing folks whom one wants to avoid having as a mate at home or office. We legally control deeds, not character.

In the case of abortion we are dealing with a specific deed. If the deed is murder, then that would seem to be a serious social concern calling for legal action, and the anti-abortion side prevails hands down. For whatever it is worth, the previous chapter pointed out that in present-day America, abortion is *not* treated as murder even when it falls under putative criminal restriction. South Dakota's prohibitory statute indicates that in the opinion of the legislators, abortion is not a Class 1 felony murder. Church officials supported the South Dakota law, but perhaps they were only playing the politics of compromise until public opinion would support harsher penalties. At the USCCB meeting following the 2008 presidential election, several bishops called for the Church to adopt a "prophetic" stance in order to oppose President-elect Obama's pro-choice views. Prophetism does not sound like political compromise. Given the tone of the USCCB meeting and the entrenched anti-abortion position of so many Church statements, one cannot leave the abortion issue isolated in politics even in South Dakota. Something must be said about the Catholic moral argument to discern whether broad-scale legal prohibition is necessary and ethically appropriate.

Intrinsic Evil

Catholic moral theory designates abortion as an "intrinsic evil." That sounds pretty bad. Catholic moral tradition holds that an act that is intrinsically evil is everywhere and always wrong. I agree with that view. What I do not accept is that declaring an act to be "intrinsic evil" is sufficient to determine a final decision. To conclude that some action is intrinsically evil does not in itself determine that it ought not to be done. Why? Because any particular action—say, abortion—cannot be isolated from the context and conditions in terms of which the final decision is made. Catholic moral theory tends to think that moral problems can be resolved without remainder. That view slights moral dilemmas and the reality of tragic choice. Tragic choice is tragic because one chooses to commit an intrinsically evil act to avoid an even greater moral evil or to accomplish an overriding "intrinsic good."

Abortion is an intrinsic evil but it may have to be chosen when facing a tragic dilemma. Abortion is not a tragedy of empire, but it is tragic none the same. Choosing abortion while failing at some level to appreciate its tragic character is a failure of moral judgment. Avishai Margalt, in a book with the provocative title *On Compromise and Rotten Compromise*, makes my point: "We should, I believe, be judged by our compromises more than by our ideals and norms. Ideals tell us something important about what we would like to be. But compromises tell us who we are." Abortion as intrinsic evil states a norm. Tragic or trivial choice for abortion tells us who we are.

There are three problems with labeling an action intrinsically evil: (1) how do you *know* that an action is an intrinsic evil, (2) how *serious* is an intrinsic evil, and (3) how does one balance intrinsic evils and intrinsic goods in determining a moral course of action? Unfortunately, there are no simple answers to any of these questions.

Artificial contraception is on the Catholic list of intrinsic evils. Maybe that is the correct view but, as noted, most Catholics by a wide margin don't seem to consider it evil at all. Intrinsic evil is clearly not, then, *obvious* evil. Even if one grants that abortion is an "intrinsic evil," does that dictate the sort of high rhetoric and stringent legal demands of the pro-life position? Not necessarily. Characterizing an action as intrinsic evil is only one aspect of moral decision-making and not the last word. As one learned monsignor put it to me, "intrinsic evil is not intrinsic sin."

What does it mean to say that an action is intrinsically evil? It means that the evil of the act is "on its face"; it is inherent in what is done, not merely in its consequences. Lying is an act that is intrinsically evil. Does that mean that one should never lie? No, but if you lie, you need a moral context that excuses the lie. The standard case is when you lie to protect Jews in the attic from the Gestapo at the door. The importance of *intrinsic* evil lies in the rejection of an alternative theory of morality: "the end justifies the means." In that theory means are morally neutral; all the value is determined by the end. For a morality of "the means justifies the end," lying is not intrinsically evil (or good)—it all depends on the results. In contrast, a morality of intrinsic evil demands a moral excuse for lying; lying is just not to be done, it is an intrinsically bad thing to do. "I know that lying is morally wrong, but in this case it was justified," not "What's the matter with lying considering the good results that came from it!"

The distinction between moral value inherent in certain acts and the morality of means and ends is crucial for understanding the nature of moral argument. Pro-lifers often accuse pro-choicers of relying on means-justify-the-end morality: the abortion is morally neutral and fully justified because it leads to a good result. If that is the basic moral theory of pro-choice, pro-life wins at the theoretical level. Pro-choice should be rejected because it is based on faulty moral theory. Means-ends morality fails because it can legitimate committing an obviously horrendous act to accomplish a good end. The standard example: torturing a child if the act somehow led to widespread happiness. Moral intuition suggests that torturing children is an intrinsic evil so abhorrent that it cannot be justified by good results. It is the *weight* of evil that makes torturing abhorrent.

The torture example can lead, however, to an overwrought reading of the morality of intrinsic evil. One can come to the wrong conclusion that once an act is judged to be an intrinsic evil, everything is decided. You must never do what is intrinsically evil! This is the underlying assumption of the rhetoric of the anti-abortion advocates. As suggested by the example of lying, the notion that intrinsic evil is never to be done does not conform to our common moral views. We may know perfectly well that lying is intrinsically evil, but judge that it is the moral thing to do in order to avoid an even greater evil. Moral deliberation demands *weighing* goods and evils prior to making a decision. The torture example is misleading because the act is so appalling that we believe that nothing could outweigh the evil of the action. When weighing moral options, torturing children is "off the scale."

An exaggerated reading of "intrinsic evil" can lead to the false impression that the general Catholic moral tradition takes no account of circumstance and consequence; there is no "weighing" of goods and evils. Not so. Catholic moral assessment of social and political issues is very much attuned to weighing good and evil. Catholic "just war" theory is a case in point. Unhappily, in the area of sexual morality—abortion included—weighing good and evil seems to be precluded. Abortion seems as much off the scale as torturing children. I will attempt to deescalate that view of abortion.

The anti-abortion argument is actually making *two* moral claims about abortion. Abortion is an intrinsic evil *and* it is of such moral weight that it may never be allowed. Catholic morality recognizes the "lesser of two evils" approach, but in the abortion debate intrinsic evil has been inflated so that that designation alone determines the gravity of the offense. Abortion may well be intrinsically evil—I think that it is—but the equation of abortion with murder, genocide, or the torture of children suggests a *weight* of evil that needs separate and differing justification. Weighing evil and good is the business of practical wisdom, which, because it depends on experience, is an ongoing task that cannot be summed in syllogisms.

Contradictory Conduct

How does the Catholic moral tradition decide that an action is intrinsically evil? Popular Catholic morality has a number of actions that are regarded as intrinsic evils; artificial contraception, homosexuality, euthanasia, and stem cell research are repeatedly condemned in this fashion. Do these items deserve the intrinsic evil designation? If one tests common opinion, there are many people who would reject the idea that any of the items on this list are evil in any way whatsoever. In some cases, rather than evil, they are goods to be pursued. Not even all Catholics accept the whole list as intrinsically evil or evil at all. Catholics who have homosexual children resist the notion that the behavior of their gay sons or daughters is an intrinsic evil leading the unfortunate offspring straight to eternal damnation.

Given the discrepancy between the official teaching about intrinsic evil, strong opposition to the teaching in secular society, and rejection by lots of people in the pews, one can wonder how the list was determined. This is not a trivial problem. To clarify matters—at least as far as that is possible—one must look further at the nature of moral reasoning and the special cast of Catholic moral philosophy.

Any moral philosophy has the task of illuminating how to discriminate good and evil. It would be useful if there was some easy and generally accepted check list of negative traits that would infallibly locate intrinsic evil, but the sheer fact of moral controversy about the issues listed above suggests that no such test is at hand. There are, however, philosophical arguments that actually do work to locate at least some intrinsic evils. These arguments compare the evil of certain actions to the falsity of certain statements. "This circle is square" is false and *intrinsically* false because it is self-contradictory: the *meaning* of "circle" precludes its being square. Lying is evil and *intrinsically* evil because it is speech that contradicts speech. Speech has a basic function to convey truth. Once we catch out the liar, he destroys his ability to use speech. In the case of "the boy who cried wolf," we are unable to tell whether he is telling the truth, lying, reciting a poem, or indulging in any of the varied ways of speech. His speech has become useless—he is speechless.

Natural Law

A strategy of self-contradiction is present in conventional Catholic natural law ethics, the philosophical position often used to derive the list of intrinsic evils above. The self-contradiction in natural law ethics is not as straightforward as in the case of lying. What is contradicted is not a "logical" connection, but a biological consequence. Sex is a biological process for procreation, so contraception and homosexuality contradict sexuality. Nurturing embryos in the womb and the death of the human body are natural process contradicted by abortion and euthanasia.

Does this natural law argument work to locate intrinsic evil? For good or for ill, it doesn't seem to be all that persuasive to a great many ordinary folks. One would like to think that *intrinsic* evils are all like torture, so obvious that everyone would agree straight off about their wickedness. The fact that there is disagreement is not, of course, the last word. Human societies and individuals have been broadly and terribly wrong about moral issues such as slavery. Nevertheless, lack of agreement about obvious wickedness should give the Catholic apologist pause. Why aren't these natural law arguments persuasive?

When it comes to philosophers—even Catholic philosophers—arguments deriving ethical norms from natural process are broadly rejected for strictly logical reasons. Such "natural law" arguments fail because they leap from a factual description to a moral prescription. True enough, sexuality is a process that can produce children, but does the biological fact dictate a moral obligation? In technical philosophy the move from description to prescription is called "the naturalistic fallacy." Because nature *happens* to act in this way, is it morally required that humans *ought* to act in that way? It doesn't seem to be a necessary conclusion. There was a time when church officials were suspicious of vaccines because they interfered with the natural process of disease and death.

Natural Good

There is a more cogent version of Catholic "natural law" ethics; it is better described not as a theory of natural *law* but of natural *goods*, or, to use the term in the abortion debate, *intrinsic* goods. A natural or intrinsic good is some action or state that does not need to be justified by some further good, just as an intrinsic evil does not wait upon results to test its value. If questioned about why you want to be healthy, the only reply would seem to be "What do you mean!" Health is good in itself and does not need to be justified by some further good. Having set forth various intrinsic goods, Catholic moralists from the Vatican on down argue that it is always and in every case an intrinsic evil to act against an intrinsic good. The poster child for this argument is the argument against contraceptives. Having children is a natural, intrinsic good. That seems correct. One should be properly baffled by the misanthrope who wonders why having children is at all a good thing. If having children is a natural good, then blocking that good by using contraceptives is immoral. Q.E D.

The difficulty with the ethics of natural or intrinsic goods occurs at a different part of the moral life: not with *identifying* good and evil, but with *balancing* good and evil in some particular situation. Natural good theory is correct in arguing that rejecting an intrinsic good as "good" is irrational. A couple might refrain from having children for various reasons, but not because they thought children were an intrinsically bad idea. The real problem in the ethics of natural goods is practical, not theoretic. What happens when realizing natural good A comes at the cost of negating natural good B? What if the natural good of having children conflicts with the natural good of the woman's health? In the controversial encyclical *Humanae Vitae* forbidding artificial contraception, Paul VI was correct in claiming that a contraceptive *mentality* is intrinsically evil, but it does not follow that an individual choice to use contraceptives to space children for the woman's health is intrinsically evil. (I won't go at all into the intricacies of arguing the essential moral difference between artificial contraception and the Church's approval of "natural family planning." To most people—Catholics included—this seems to be a distinction without a difference.) The fact that natural goods conflict is an all too frequent fact of everyday life. It is clearly the issue in the abortion debate.

Conflicts between moral goods and evils are real and not solved by formula. It is important, however, to mention one way in which Catholic philosophers deal with ethical dilemma. John Finnis, a distinguished and conservative natural good theorist, says that we may not choose to contradict any natural good because in God's plan natural goods are compatible. True enough, there is no *inherent* contradiction between having children and a healthy mother, but in actual life situations it isn't logical compatibility but practical incompatibility that is the problem. God may be able to create and sustain all goods simultaneously, but humans can't manage the trick, and so we are burdened with weighing good and evil in deciding what to do. I mention Finnis's argument not because it seems to me very helpful, but because both standard Catholic natural law and natural good arguments have a tendency to lapse into theology. Take a strong enough view of God as the designer of nature and frustration of his sexual mechanics is like abusing the tools in your workshop. Assume that God has it all arranged that in the long run all good will be realized simultaneously, and one ought not to frustrate the divine intent. Whatever the use of such arguments for theologians, they will not carry the day in the secular debate about abortion.

One should not overstate the failure of natural law or natural good ethics to be decisive for the moral life. We may not be able to read duties from our DNA or manage to realize simultaneous natural goods, but it would be irrational if we did not in moral deliberation take account of the facts of human biology or seek to realize as many goods as possible. Natural good theory is very useful in getting an initial fix on the morality of abortion. It would be bizarre for someone to believe that having an abortion was one of life's natural or intrinsic goods. As an adolescent a young woman may look forward to all sorts of prospective goods, from being able to drive a car to completing a college education. She is not, however, looking forward to the time when she can have an abortion. The decision to have an abortion is taken because the woman believes that something has gone wrong that needs correction. Remedying the wrong inherently involves a problematic moral choice. Because the fetus has moral weight, its destruction demands moral regret or repentance. One does not place either regret or immorality as one of life's goals. While it sounds harsh, abortion *is* an intrinsic evil, though one that may be licit or even required, given other serious moral considerations. That at least would seem to be a moral assessment which commands broad allegiance.

Morals as Natural

While some actions can be labeled intrinsic evils because they are "self-contradictory," like lying, and some pursuits are intrinsically good because they are so obvious for human flourishing, there remains a large domain of acts and goals about which there is no logical or intuitive means of reaching agreement. One might cite the moral standing of women as an example. I choose this example because the status of women is a critical factor in the abortion controversy.

In some societies it seems obvious that women are entitled to full moral sovereignty over their lives; in others they remain constricted because they are judged incapable of making a full range of practical decisions. Rather like children, women have some rights but they are "protected" by males who know better what is good for women. In Western societies, women by and large are currently regarded to be as morally capable as men, though less than a century ago in many of these same societies women were not allowed to vote because of presumed political disabilities. Why did matters change? Why do people in Western societies regard the status assigned to women by, say, the Taliban as obviously immoral? There may be various general theories for asserting moral equality of the sexes, but I would suggest that it has been the lessons of experience that have brought about the change and the conviction. In the nineteenth century in the United States, women were not allowed to receive higher education. It was believed that their constitutions could not withstand the rigors of exacting research. When by persistence a few women were admitted—some had to sit in the hallway outside the classroom so as not to diminish the high male culture within—it turned out that women could do physics, be surgeons, and learn Greek.

Much of our common moral agreement on good and evil has emerged from individuals and societies being open to actual experience beyond the presumed hard and fast conclusions of elegant moral theory or religious commands. Moral advance occurs when there is openness to the sensitive experience of others. We share our life stories and experience; we discover new values and common ground. One of the most depressing byproducts of the abortion debate is the closure to experience that strident advocacy has produced.

A final word on natural law: "natural law" does not define a standard moral position. There are various competing and conflicting "natural law" theories. For the argument of this book, the most interesting are the natural law arguments of the great Catholic theologians of the Middle Ages. Their appeal to natural law is unlike either the standard natural law arguments used by Church officials or the natural good theories. Classic medieval "natural law" rests on the view that *morality is natural to human beings*. Ethics is not something imposed on human nature by custom or ruling elites; morality is an intrinsic activity of human nature because moral reasoning is natural to human beings. *Moral* reasoning is not, however, the *theoretical* reason of science wherein we expect definitive universal demonstration. Confusion of moral and scientific reason, as I hope to demonstrate below, leads to a misplaced understanding of the sense in which morality can be "objective." Most particularly, the medieval view does *not* provide us with an infallible code of morals. One of the most astute students of medieval natural law, Jean Porter at Notre Dame, puts it succinctly: "The natural law does not provide us with a system of ethical norms which is detailed enough to be practical and compelling to all rational and well disposed persons." The modesty of the medieval construction of natural morality can be commended to both sides of the abortion debate. It opens up moral argument to the complexity of our continuing, often changing, experience and the lessons of practical wisdom.

Gut Decisions

Self-contradictory conduct, natural goods, and shared experience may be able to locate certain goods and evils, but that will not cover all the aspects of moral assessment and decision. Even if we agree on goods and evils, we are still left with the problem of actually making decisions under conditions of conflict and complexity. The moral field can present so many conflicting goods and evils, be so full of passionate advocacy, that we will be tempted at the point of final decision to abandon argument altogether. We make "gut decisions" to end all argument. The danger is that gut decisions easily infect the whole deliberative process, reducing moral argument to trading tastes. Take that route in the abortion debate, so fraught with contradictory claims, and some sort of pro-choice wins by default. The only thing one can finally conclude is that people do choose one way or another.

The clearly wrong conclusion from the existence of passionate ethical controversy about abortion is that moral argument does not work because it is an impossible enterprise: moral judgment is through and through individual and subjective—it does not rest on rational considerations. It is gut decisions all the way down. Pro-life and pro-choice "arguments" are merely expressions of likes and dislikes. I disapprove of abortion, she approves. "Subjectivism" of this sort has been the *bête noire* of John Paul II and Benedict XVI. For these learned pontiffs, moral subjectivism is the besetting sin of the modern world. What is needed is a return to ethical objectivity. The popes are correct to reject a subjectivism of any old choice, but it is not clear what they mean by moral "objectivity." Since it is comforting in a text critical of Catholic moral doctrine to agree wholeheartedly with the pope, let me deal with the failure of ethical skepticism.

Some serious philosophers do argue for the utter subjectivity of morality, but it is difficult to take these serious philosophers seriously. Whatever the power of their argument, people continue to dispute about moral issues as if there was some truth to be had. The fact that moral arguments persist despite the sober warnings of the philosophers should be conclusive enough, but the subjectivist position is ultimately self-contradictory, which, as already noted, is always a bad way to argue. The whole point of writing a philosophical treatise arguing for the subjectivity of morals is to make a moral point. The subjectivist thinks that people *ought* to stop arguing about morals and, by the way, not take up swords and cudgels to enforce their (ahem!) "moral" views. In short, the subjectivist seeks to eliminate morals for a deep moral purpose: stop fighting! If the subjectivist were correct in his theory, then his arguments would have no effect. My subjective liking for "moral" combat is not for a moment swayed by the philosopher's subjective dislike of "moral" conflict.

Subjectivizing the moral issue of abortion won't work for just such reasons. Pro-choice advocates do not want to subjectivize morality because they want to make a moral demand on the pro-lifer: "It is immoral to oppose pro-choice because your opposition only expresses a personal dislike of abortion. One *ought not* to condemn people for their likes and dislikes. Back off!" At a deeper level, it is difficult to accept the notion that abortion is a matter of likes and dislikes. It is true that I do not have to justify my taste for bitter chocolate, but it would be quite unacceptable for a woman to say that she had an abortion because she liked the procedure or had a taste for the experience. As argued above, abortion is an "intrinsic evil" at least in the minimal sense that it cannot be one of life's intrinsically desirable goods. Abortion is undertaken only because something has gone wrong, and that is its moral justification, if it has any.

Objective Morality?

There is always one moral demand, then, in a subjectivist's argument: don't fuss about morals. This is a pretty limited morality, but it has one value: tolerance. While tolerance is in many cases a virtue and a strategy, it is not plausible as the only moral injunction. There are horrendous deeds that should not be tolerated. What is the alternative to moral skepticism? John Paul II and Benedict XVI claim we need "objective" moral standards. But what is *moral* objectivity? The popes and Catholic moral theory are correct in thinking that there are actions and states of life which are intrinsically good and some that are intrinsically evil. We have even learned from experience: for centuries Church authorities approved of and even practiced slavery. The puzzling issue is not whether there are objective goods and evils, however derived, but whether *moral deliberation* can be objective. Faced with some mix of objective goods and evils, how I sort and weigh them can seem a matter of subjective determination. Not quite, but the plausibility of subjective morality stems in part from a mistaken view of "objective" morality.

Objectivity in moral deliberation and decision is often misunderstood as if it were like scientific objectivity. In science we understand how to deal with a complex particular situation through the application of various laws. If you want to land a rocket at a particular spot on the moon, you specify the relative positions of the launch and landing site, the weight and thrust of the vehicle, calculate from the laws of gravity, and so on to understand how to accomplish that precise end. In moral decision, one might think that you can bring to bear relevant moral laws that will determine the exact and proper action. Deduction from laws seems to be a common model for science and morals. In moral reasoning this deductive exercise is called "casuistry"; it is the stock-in-trade of the legal world. But there is an essential difference between scientific deduction and moral or legal casuistry.

Deduction from scientific law is conclusive: the case at hand must perfectly exemplify the law. In the physical law of falling bodies, we expect this particular falling body to comply fully with the equations which measure the rate of descent. If the case deviates in any way, we discount the deviation by introducing extraneous factors like friction. By way of contrast, in moral and legal casuistry we are trying to discover if *this* case does actually fall under the law. In science we deduce the case as an *instance* of the law; in morals we decide the case is an *interpretation* of the law. In the courts, case law is an essential part of the process. Cases in a sense *determine the law by interpretation.* Cases can "change" the law by expansion or contraction. Interpretation proceeds not by deduction but by analogy; this case is sufficiently *like* some other case so that it is rational to group them together as a proper interpretation of the law. Modern philosophers like to differentiate items that are identical from those grouped by "family resemblance." Moral cases under law may not be identical, but they should have a family resemblance to one another. Seeking family resemblance and arguing from analogy are perfectly rational modes of argument—they are just not strict deduction.

The deductive model of objective moral law and cases seems highly plausible, but it cannot work with the precision required for a moon landing. It is the failure to make this small but vital distinction between scientific and ethical "objectivity" that makes the popes' advocacy of "objective" morality obscure. There is a truth in morality, but ethics is not physics. Put another way, moral deliberation is not a theoretical science—thus the subtitle of this chapter, "not too much theory." Reasoning by analogy is more an art than a science, but for all that it is as rational as the subject matter allows. It can even be conclusive. The end point of moral deliberation is not deductive certainty or subjective opinion, it is practical wisdom.

The Art of Moral Deliberation

If moral deliberation is more of an art than a science, then it is instructive to consider how reasoning proceeds in the evaluation of art. There is no objective science for separating the beautiful from the trash. Because artistic evaluation lacks deductive rules, many people regard artistic appraisal as nothing more than subjective opinion and individual taste. Subjectivists often regard moral judgments as if they were mere expressions of taste. This is a false view of both morality and art. Subjectivity and taste may be enough for the casual listener or stroller through the gallery, but it is not true for those who are deeply into an artistic practice.

One of our daughters is a classical violinist married to a composer. They "know" that there is a real difference between good music and bad music. How do they "know"? Compositions or performances are placed alongside one another. They play it, listen to it, compare it, live with it, and they conclude with certainty that *this* work has great musical value. Of course, even practitioners may quarrel—just how good is Sibelius, after all?—but quarrels among dedicated practitioners operate at a level of insight and understanding that transforms their back and forth arguments from expressions of taste to the level of rational consideration. Though there are no laws above from which one can deduce that this particular painting is worthy, artistic evaluation has a highly developed vocabulary that guides discussion. This vocabulary has some of the function of laws in scientific understanding. In the evaluation of painting it is important to look for order and design. In music we look to proper tempo and expression.

In many essentials, moral deliberation proceeds in the same pattern as the appraisals of serious art critics and practitioners. The art connoisseur and the morally wise are individuals who have long and deep acquaintance with the particular artistic or moral practice. (This is why the morally and spiritually wise are so often depicted as individuals of great age. Young people have moral enthusiasms; the aged, we fancy, have acquired wisdom.) In the case of art, the critic must know the history of the art in its many variations and styles. The "expert" in moral deliberation is deeply immersed in human history, in moral cases, in actual moral life in all its variability. It is from broad and deep experience in the experience of life that moral deliberation is refined and enriched beyond a deductive model. The wise person "knows" from experience that this mix of intrinsic goods and evils is the moral course, and that one is ill-conceived.

Moral subjectivists may regard moral argument as mere expression of likes but, as with the artistic evaluation, I suspect that they aren't actually much engaged with the practices under discussion. Morality may look subjective from the philosopher's study carrel, but it seldom seems so on the street. It is always interesting in a beginning ethics course, filled with sophisticated college sophomores fully dedicated to ethical subjectivism, to announce that grades will be assigned by throwing the exams down the stairs. Those that travel farthest flunk and so on up the stairs and the grade level. Moral protest is the immediate reaction. A little actual engagement in justice creates a passion for "objective" morality.

Moral "objectivists" often seem to be disengaged from practice on the abortion issue. Laying down the law in print or the pulpit is one thing. Contrast preaching, however, with the story told to me by a university chaplain. The chaplain, a woman and former Catholic, talked about the importance of listening to the troubled pregnancy stories of the young women she counseled. For this chaplain, abortion was not a theoretical argument in a catechism—it was an anguished conversation in her office as the woman she was counseling struggled to arrive at a difficult and morally significant decision about her life. The chaplain did not believe that any old choice would do, she was not a "subjectivist," but she was convinced that deductive arguments from abstract law bypassed the reality of moral conversation, decision, and practice—bypassed the lived experience of the individual young woman in her office.

Moral deliberation is an art developed from deep life experience as well as imagining ourselves into other lives through history, biography, and sensitive literature. Sufficient moral deliberation will even lead to identifying "objective" goods that must be pursued, as well as "objective" faults to be avoided. The problem is that, like practicing the violin, composing a quartet, or evaluating the latest modernist concerto, it takes a lot of time, effort, and insight. Simplifying morality is tempting because, while we may wait for time and history to sort out the *real* artistic masterpieces, moral decisions cannot be postponed. What do I do *now*! Because of the urgency of moral decision, having a simple model for decision is fatally attractive. There are two attractive simplifications for morality: gut subjectivism and deductive objectivism. Choose what you like *or* here is a simple deduction from a moral law. Both strategies degrade moral deliberation. Of course, moral decisions must be made and made now, but there is an obligation to be as comprehensive as possible in understanding the complexity we face. We cannot achieve categorical deductive certainty, but we can strive to make wise judgments.

Moral Wisdom and Experience

Moral wisdom comes finally from experience but experience is not passive observation. After all, people often have experiences, or are in the midst of experiences, that they utterly fail to understand. The divorce courts would suggest that all too many people experience sex and marriage but so misunderstand the emotional and moral ranges of what they have undergone that they abandon the task. Conversely, a sensitive poet or novelist may capture the inner essence of a life from the most fragmentary clues. The great novelist Henry James wrote a review of a book on "how to write a novel." The well-intentioned author recommended that authors write "from experience." James thought that a commendable idea, but then went on to note the case of an author friend who had written a splendid novel about French Protestant youth—a rather rare breed. Having shown deep understanding of that special culture, it was assumed that the author must have had extensive experience with such young people. Not at all. Evidently she had been staying in an apartment house when, on descending the stairs one day, she glanced into an open door where a religious meeting was taking place. Passing right by, something about the dress, the posture, and social interchange she observed in that fleeting experience opened up the sensibilities of the group and became the center from which she spun her tale. She brought to her momentary glance a complex experience of human gesture and attitudes, a spider web of sensibilities into which her observation was located, connected, and enriched.

Poetry and fiction are not the only means of building the sort of sensitivity that can, almost at a glance, perceive the deep truth of life. Knowledge of history and biography sets forth patterns of human complexity that enrich moral deliberation. Even philosophy, when not too absorbed in its own technical apparatus, connects and illuminates the multiple ways of humankind. Deep experience, however derived, is necessary for developing moral wisdom. It is all too easy to note the event and miss the experience. The gap between passive awareness and deep experience is particularly an issue in the intimacy of sexuality and the topic of this book: pregnancy.

Theology of the Body

The complexity of deep experience must not be confused with philosophical complexity or scholarly density. Pope John Paul II's lectures, collected in the work titled *Theology of the Body,* are as logically tangled and dense as anyone could possibly wish. Even defenders of the pope's views admit that the text is daunting. Yet I would contend that the work misses the experience he sets out to understand and hence fails as an exercise in practical wisdom about sexuality. Despite the pope's training in the specialized branch of philosophy called "phenomenology," his treatment misses the very *phenomenon* of the human body. The title itself is misleading because the focus of the book is human sexuality; the text almost totally ignores all the rest of the body. The body does a lot of other things besides have sex—it gets sick, experiences puberty, practices tennis or the violin, gets old, and so on. Even in the matter of sex, the other states of the body cannot be discounted.

When the pope turns to sexuality, the analysis seems peculiarly "theoretical" and abstract. The essence of proper sexuality is, he asserts, "mutual self-giving." There is something correct about that. We can all understand that something is wrong with sexual intercourse that is forced overtly in rape, or covertly in manipulative seduction. It is not clear that these are even cases of sex; it is often alleged that rape is about power, and the sex is only a symbol of dominance. The problem with "self-giving" is the elusiveness of "self"—just who am I, what is the self that I can give, do I have enough self to give? For many years standard Catholic marital advice to women—especially to women—was to sacrifice themselves in marriages that were difficult and even abusive. Unhappily, following this line of advice often led not to the woman *giving* of herself, but to her *obliterating* of herself—becoming a passive nothing. In the parlance of the street: a punching bag. Self-giving is only valuable if there is a robust sense of self-worth to give. (Self-giving wrongly understood as "passivity" is also a fault line in the Church's understanding of abortion, as I will try to show in the next chapter.) John Paul's "self-giving" extends beyond the mutuality of sexual union to the self-giving of the parents in being open to conceiving a child in every instance—thus the condemnation of contraception.

Beyond the clearly pernicious interpretation of self-giving as self-obliteration, there is the significant problem of realizing the pope's lofty sexual goal in ordinary life. We are, after all, imperfect "selves" encumbered by all the quirks of person and circumstance. Everyday sexuality has an experiential density that can make "mutual self-giving" seem remote. Sex occurs in the midst of life: I am tired tonight, the kids may not be asleep, I have a tough day tomorrow, my mother is sick, we might not be able to afford another child. Did I manage to "give" myself in the midst of such daily distractions? Sex is just not simple bodily congress; it is often obscure on the psychic self-giving side. No wonder strict moralists from St. Augustine to Immanuel Kant have thought that sex has an inherent sinfulness because of the inherent selfishness. For Augustine the only way to avoid sinful sex is to have none of it! There is something troubling in a sexual ethic that cannot be realized.

The pope's theology of the body reminds me of a story told about the great virtuoso Paganini. He was in the midst of a performance when a string broke on his violin. The master clawed at the other strings until only one remained. He finished the concert, held up the damaged instrument, and exulted, "Paganini and one string!" John Paul's theology of the body and Catholic commentators on sexuality are like Paganini with one string. It is an extraordinary technical achievement, but it is not how the violin is meant to be played. You can play the human body on one conceptual string, but playing the violin or the body with only one string limits the repertoire.

Chapter Four

Rights, Persons, and Pregnancy

Deliberating about the morality of abortion in the conflicting circumstances of life is not a simple task, but it is not so complex that we should throw up our hands and give it over to fancy or feeling. Abortion requires thoughtful moral evaluation by individuals and society; it asks for practical wisdom. In preparation for writing this book, I reviewed a good bit of the philosophical literature, both pro and con, about abortion. The various authors offered probative and ingenious arguments for one or another view of the moral standing of the fetus, the conditions of the pregnancy, the woman's social and economic circumstances, and so on. All of the discussants latched on to some important part of the abortion question, but my overall impression was that most ended their presentations without covering the full moral situation attendant on individual pregnancies.

The abortion story from the initiating sexual event through the actual situation of the pregnancy on to birth presents many conflicting and diverse factors for moral consideration. Pro-choice and pro-life both capture a slice of that dense reality. Depending on the factors chosen, their moral assessments will vary dramatically. Finally, however, the morality of an abortion decision needs to be discussed in the full mix of physical, psychological, social, cultural, and economic conditions of the pregnant woman, the cause of the pregnancy (consensual, rape, incest, failure of contraception), the status of the fetus at various stages, the role of legal rights, moral compassion, the culture of an abortion-on-demand society, and so on. Pro-life urges carrying to term and putting the child up for adoption. Is that a real possibility both in terms of the social or ethnic conditions of the woman? Not all babies from all racial groups are well positioned for adoption. There may be serious hesitation about adopting children who come from women who have led troubled lives—not an insignificant number among those seeking abortion. Ultimate religious views will also enter the equation, but not as directly as the pro-life proponents suggest. The dominant pro-choice and pro-life arguments tell us something about the abortion dilemma at the price of simplification.

I have divided this chapter into three main sections that address central terms in the abortion debate: "Rights," "Persons," and "Pregnancy." The three concepts are linked in complex ways that either support or deny the moral or legal legitimacy of abortion. "Rights" and "persons" have been particularly prominent in the debates, while "pregnancy" has been more a passive fact that raises the question of rights and persons. I want to argue that the life experience of pregnancy is determinative in assessing the moral situation. Only if one understands the full reality of the "pregnant person" can the assignment of rights and the status of the "fetal person" be assessed.

RIGHTS

Living on Rights

The most obvious simplification in the abortion debate is that both sides frame the issue as a clash of *rights*: right to life, right to choose. I am not original in pointing out the limitation of rights talk, but it is worth repeating. Rights are a persuasive tool in American political discourse. As a first line of attack or a last ditch defense, we stand on our rights! Rights talk has its place, but enclosing the moral life in rights talk is counterproductive. Marriage is a complex moral relation but when married couples resort to standing on their rights, the divorce court is only one step away. The power and limitation of rights talk in the abortion debate is exemplified in a famous article, "In Defense of Abortion," by philosopher Judith Jarvis Thompson. Thompson fancies a situation in which I awaken one morning to discover that I have been kidnapped in the night by a society of music lovers. I find myself in a hospital where my kidneys are attached to the failing kidneys of a world-class violinist. I am told that if I unhook the tubes, the maestro will die. I am assured that after nine months he will recover, and we can be detached. As an analogy to pregnancy, Thompson's bizarre tale is illuminating. She grants that the violinist is a person with a right to life and, for purpose of her argument, Thompson is willing to grant the pro-life claim that the fetus is a person with a right to life. Question: does the violinist have a *right* to the use of my kidneys? I think her answer is correct: he does not have a *right* to the use of my body, even if it means that by unhooking he will die. Conclusion: merely noting that the fetus has a right to life does not as such close the argument.

Thompson's argument shows a limitation in the standard pro-life argument. The fact that some other person has a right to life does not in itself establish that I have the obligation to sustain that life. The other must have, as she says, a "right against me," and that implies some appraisal of my history relative to the other person. Common moral judgment suggests that having been kidnapped and hooked up to the violinist against my will does not establish the maestro's "right against me." Presumably, this is the reason that many people believe that abortion after rape is permissible. If, as in the South Dakota law, abortion is permissible for pregnancy after rape, the assumption is that a "right against the woman" has not been established.

Is Thompson's fictitious case sufficient to capture all the moral dimensions of abortion—or the violinist problem, for that matter? No, and Thompson is the first to point this out. Even if one is clear about rights, that does not by itself settle *what I ought to do*. There are many facts we would want to know before deciding on the proper moral action. Different facts will tilt the moral compass one way or another. How did I get into this fix? How are matters supposed to develop? The situation would be different if I had signed a contract to loan my kidneys for nine months. Was there a clause in the contract that allowed me to unplug if I begin to suffer significant medical or psychological distress?

In the kidnap scenario, what if the hook-up is not nine months, but only a week? The violinist still has no *right* to use my body, but it would be callous of me to unhook him. If a week suggests I exercise compassion, how about two weeks, or a month? There is no clear cutoff, but one would probably judge that at some point—two years?—what is called for is not simple decency, but heroism and saintliness. Bravo for dedication above and beyond the call of duty, but it is *beyond the call of duty*. Neither law nor morality can command saintliness. Where is the dividing line between duty and moral heroism in an individual pregnancy? Pro-life accusations of abortion as gravely immoral need to consider whether, in certain cases, carrying a pregnancy through to term demands saintliness. Saintliness is not a moral duty.

Thompson is correct that simply asserting the fetus's right to life does not settle the abortion question. Complicate the circumstances in certain ways and our moral judgment may override any such "right." In the violinist case, we would judge one way if there was prior consent and contract. On the other hand, if I was forced at gunpoint to hook my kidneys to the violinist, I would judge that he had no right to use me thus. It would take magnanimity of a high order not to pull the plug in indignation. Finally, there is the issue of compassion and how far that may carry moral decision. The general point is that moral decisions about pregnancy and abortion involve moral considerations beyond a direct contest of rights.

Doing the Right Thing

Part of the confusion about "rights" in the abortion debate is that "rights" are so often evoked as a convenient word for designating the moral thing to do even though there is no strict "right" involved. We often say that something is "the right thing to do" even when there are no rights at issue. Thompson offers a clear example. A rich uncle gives a box of candy to two nephews and tells them to share. The older boy hogs the candy. He is denying the younger brother a right. Contrast: the rich uncle gives a box of candy to the older boy. Again he hogs down the chocolates, refusing to share with his brother, who is at least as fond of sweets as the elder. Hogging the candy is not the right thing to do, but the younger brother has not been denied candy that is his by right. It may be the right thing to do to carry the fetus to term, but not from the direct claim that the fetus has a right to life.

In the candy case, the issue is not rights but the right thing to do, the obligation that we have to do good. It is important to recognize the difference between claims in justice and those of benevolence. The violinist may have no claim in justice for the use of my kidneys, but I may have an obligation in benevolence to help him out as the circumstances suggest. In the abortion case, the fetus may have no claim in justice, no right to the use of the woman's body, but she may have an obligation in benevolence toward this nascent life. Obligation in benevolence is real enough, but benevolence is not an obligation for moral heroism.

A last word on "rights" talk. There is some justification for noting that a demand for rights is a part of what has been called "the male imaginary." Males like to construct moral situations as a decisive contest between clearly separate parties asserting their rights. Women, it is claimed with some justification, are more relational in their dealing with others. Self and other are not so clearly separated. The woman may find it more appropriate to reach out in compassion to the other, to try to understand the other, than simply stand on her rights. I would not want to pursue this line too far, suggesting utter gender determinism in moral argument, but the special situation of pregnancy—an experience that only women can know—involves something closer to mutual relationship between the woman and her fetus than a contestation of separate beings over their respective rights. This intimate relation of the woman and her fetus is, in my judgment, the essential consideration in the abortion debate.

Persons

Human Beings

Nothing is more fundamental to the good of a person than life itself. However the woman may have become pregnant, she is in a vital biological relation to the other. The relation between the woman and her fetus is not the relation I have to the violinist or a faraway South American peasant who, of course, clearly has "a right to life." I have no relation to the peasant beyond common humanity. I might send a contribution to CARE, but it would be missionary heroism to fly to his side. Pro-life will insist that the biological relation establishes "a right against the woman" such that she is morally compelled to carry the fetus to term no matter the pain and distress. The fact that carrying a child to term may, in some circumstances, be more than a moral obligation and move over into moral heroism is probably not going to persuade the ardent pro-life advocate. It would be a significant advance, however, if pro-life advocates were to distinguish ordinary moral duty and saintliness. Saintliness may be a religious goal, but failing to attain such ultimate benevolence is not regarded as a moral fault or a criminal act.

The common, most effective, and most controversial pro-choice rejoinder to the pro-life claim about the woman's duty to the fetus is to deny that the fetus has any right to life because the fetus is not a "person." Pro-choice denies the equivalence between the fetus and the ailing violinist. For pro-choice, the fetus, particularly at the early stages, does not meet the criteria for personhood. Lacking complex psychological functioning, the early fetus is more like a vegetable or a lower animal than a human person. The fact that in the gestation process the human embryo reenacts evolution from primitive life on up gives biological warrant to the pro-choice claim. Not being a "person," the fetus cannot command the moral status and rights of a mature human being. Only another person may have a right against me to support life, so, if the fetus is not a person, the right to life argument fails fundamentally.

While "person" is the usual term in this debate, pro-life advocates often use a broader term: the fetus is a "human being," leaving the intricacies of high functioning "personhood" aside. Clearly the fetus is *not* a carrot or a cat—it is a *human* fetus through and through. One can leave the complexity of "person" and higher function aside and emphasize the undoubted fact that the fetus is a *human* being. It is not clear, however, just what the substitution of "human being" for "person" actually accomplishes for the moral argument. The pro-life proponent assumes that designating something as a "human being" automatically assigns moral worth—and worth of a very high order.

Talking about "human being" has obvious persuasive force but one has to recognize that the *moral* value has been implicitly *assigned* to "human being." "Human being" can be taken as simple descriptions of fact (a fetus with human DNA). The phrase "human being" in the pro-life argument is made to play two roles: descriptive and evaluative. I can ask of almost anything whether it is "human" in some factual sense. A robot may perform "human" functions but still be a machine. Any cell of the human body is a human cell. Noting that this cell is a *human* cancer cell carries no moral weight toward its preservation. When "human being" is used in the pro-choice argument it borrows its moral force from our well-established moral assignment of value to fully actualized human bodies: newborn babies, children, adults, and so on.

Even when there is clearly a developed human body, a body with human DNA, there can be disputes about moral weight. The influential philosopher Peter Singer has argued that defective newborns and demented elders may respectfully be "put to sleep." Like the fetus, they lack higher function, although they are certainly DNA-human bodies. If we regard the notion of killing off the defective and the demented as morally unacceptable, it is because we have *already* assigned a certain high value to the fact that we are dealing with something with significant moral weight, no matter how immature, defective, or demented. I think that Singer's moral position is unacceptable but that is something to be argued for rather than simply stated by proclaiming the equal moral status of "human being" in any state or condition.

It is frequently said that the issue of abortion turns on "the sanctity of human life." "Sanctity" is an elevated way of saying that human life is an "intrinsic good." I would agree that human life is an "intrinsic good," but so is life in general: animal and vegetable life. Destroying animal and vegetable life wantonly or for mere pleasure or greed is immoral. Modern environmentalists are as likely to speak of the "sanctity of nature" as the pro-life proponent is eager to speak of the sanctity of human life. As was argued in the previous chapter, noting that something is an intrinsic good is not the end of moral deliberation. We often have to weigh intrinsic goods against one another and against intrinsic evils. Even the most committed believer in the sanctity of nature will probably judge that the intrinsic good of sustaining human life outweighs the intrinsic good of plant life.

"Person"

However one wants to argue about the moral weight of "human being," "person" is the term most disputed in the abortion debate. "Person" in the abortion debate is not a simple descriptive term like "human," as in human DNA. "Person" seems already morally and legally loaded and is thus a more effective term. The "personhood" amendments offered by pro-lifers to the U.S. Constitution or Colorado demonstrate this point. "Person" has resonance as a *moral* term that "human" does not.

Unfortunately for the purpose of clarifying the abortion arguments, there have been great historical quarrels about applying the notion of "person." Arguing over the "personhood" of the fetus is only the latest controversy. There have been historic disputes about whether women, blacks, animals, and business associations are properly "persons." Or, if they are "persons," what level of moral status applies to that *sort* of person. The U.S. Constitution regarded slaves as three-fifths of a person in determining population statistics. Pro-life advocates have been quick to analogize the status of the fetus to that of Negro slaves: as it was wrong to regard a slave as less than a person, so too with the fetus. Good point, but it does suggest that legal "person" is not as obvious a designation as biological member of the human species. Slaves were regarded as human, just not assigned full legal personhood. The same might be said about how women have been regarded as "persons." In the American past, women were regarded as persons of a sort, but their moral and legal status was often radically curtailed in comparison to males. A significant ingredient in the abortion debate has been the change in perception about the status of women such that they are regarded now as enjoying the range of moral capacities and rights as males.

While it was clearly wrong to regard slaves or women as lesser persons in law, it is not obvious that the law is wrong to regard the fetus, particularly in its early stages, as less than a full legal person. In the law, an assailant who causes a woman to have a miscarriage is not charged with homicide. Pro-life advocates who advocate full personhood for the fetus from conception on have attempted to change that legal assumption, but so far they have not succeeded. Common moral opinion tends to support the law. Grievous harm has been caused to the woman, but not the murder of a person. Anyone who believes, as I do, that the fetus's moral status increases with its developmental stage holds that the fetus is something less than legal person in the earlier stages.

"There's Nobody Here But Us Persons!"

If applying "personhood" to or withdrawing it from a corporation, racial type, gender, or fetus has been disputed even by sober heads, it is because "person" is a "thin" concept. It grants some moral or legal status to the item designated, but it does not delineate exact duties. The philosopher Robert Paul Wolff wrote an interesting article with the title "There's Nobody Here But Us Persons!" Suppose I want to know what is making all that racket in the room next door. I am told it is a room full of "persons." That is thin information. It excludes a loud television set, but I would know a lot more if I am told that it is a teen rock concert, a political rally of retirees, or a terrorist attack. In these three cases I would draw different moral conclusions about the persons involved and my moral responsibilities.

In the abortion debate one could, therefore, designate that the fetus is a "person" without thereby determining the range of moral and legal obligations owed to a *fetal person*. In the course of human life, we may have significantly different moral and legal obligations to fetal, infant, teen, adult, or aged persons. Men and women are both persons, but difference in gender may require different but not demeaning moral and legal treatment. The law may guarantee female persons pregnancy leave, or exclude them from combat duty in the armed forces. Fetal persons may have a presumptive right to be carried to term, but that right may not measure up to the right of an infant to nurture and protection. The sick have a right to be cared for, but the level and urgency of care may be sharply different for a young person in otherwise robust health and an old person with serious prior debilitation. My mother died at age 107. One doctor suggested that she might benefit from a pacemaker. Neither she nor I thought that made any sense at her age and with her level of function. At fifty, it would have been the therapy of choice. Denying her that treatment would have been a serious moral failure.

Putting this into "rights" language: even if the fetal person has a "right to life," that right may not be as weighty as the "right to life" of the pregnant person—hence the usual legal permission for abortion to save the life of the mother. (I remind the reader that this is not the official Catholic position: direct abortion is always prohibited even if it is judged medically necessary or prudent to preserve the life of the mother.)

Pre-Formed Persons

There is an interesting historical lesson that is useful in evaluating the claim that the fetus is fully a person without qualification. In the seventeenth century the invention of the microscope allowed scientists for the first time to examine human sperm. The shock was that there were so many. We now estimate that the normal ejaculation contains between 20 million and 150 million sperm. Unhappily for the science and theology of the time, some scientists assumed that each of the sperm was a *homonunculus*, a tiny pre-formed human being. There are textbooks from this time with drawings of a sperm that show a small human figure encased in an elongated bubble. The female ovum was regarded literally as an "egg" whose principal function was to feed the tiny pre-formed human until it grew to proper size. This obviously raised great theological problems. Since it was recognized that only a few sperm would actually develop, what was the eternal destiny of all the other tiny pre-formed humans?

Better biology today gives the female an essential contribution to the embryo, so we don't worry about 180 million unborn humans. But this only moves the problem of "pre-formation" down the developmental line. What is the moral or theological assessment of excess embryos from in vitro fertilization or lost in spontaneous miscarriage? It is estimated that somewhere between 60 percent to 80 percent of naturally fertilized eggs never make it through to birth. How does one treat miscarriage in a manner consistent with the claim that from the moment of conception one is dealing with a full-fledged person? As one critic put it, if we gave full weight to the claim that a staggering number of persons die during pregnancy, miscarriage should be regarded as a serious public health problem. Statistics about miscarriage also severely constrict the claim made by anti-abortion advocates that forty million babies have died since *Roe* because forty million abortions have been performed. Since 90 percent plus of induced abortions occur very early in pregnancy, it is highly unlikely that the majority of the forty million would have made it to birth.

Most telling in the context of this book, the Church does not within its special ministry treat a miscarried fetus as a person deserving even a minor blessing. A priest friend was importuned by a woman waiting for in vitro fertilization to baptize the fertilized egg because it was, after all, a person and deserved a ticket into heaven. He refused. The inconsistency between the notion of the embryo or fetus as a full-fledged "person" and the legal, public health, and sacramental evaluation of miscarriage is telling. Like the slippage between abortion as murder and the legal penalty, the Church's claim for an embryonic "person" and the lack of sacramental treatment of miscarriage is inconsistent. Applying the notion of person to the fetus may be acceptable to call moral attention to developing life, but it overstates the case. Even if we admit that the fetus is a "person," we should not confuse and conflate the moral obligations to a "fetal person" with those owed to a newborn person.

Biblical Embryology

Maybe common law and common moral intuition do not raise the status of the fetus to the status of a newborn, but what about the Bible? Scripture presumably trumps all merely human law and morality. Standard Catholic anti-abortion arguments—and evangelical anti-abortion argument even more so—often rest on biblical citation: "Before I formed you in the womb, I knew you" (Jeremiah 1:4–5); "Your own hands shaped me, molded me" (Job 10:8); or "For thou didst form my inward parts—Thou didst knit me together in my mother's womb" (Psalms 139:13). These citations presumably indicate a human soul from the moment of conception.

There are three problems with such citations. First, there is the poetic language of the Bible. As one commentator points out, when Isaiah says he wishes to comfort the brokenhearted, he is not presenting himself as a cardiac surgeon. Second, the omniscient and caring Creator knows every living creature in the womb, but not all mammalian embryos are morally weighty persons. Third and finally, there are other passages that send a different message. In Old Testament law (Exodus 21:22–25) there is a careful distinction between the life of a mother and the life of her fetus. If, in an altercation, a woman suffers a miscarriage, the aggressor is to be fined; if the woman is killed, "you shall give life for life." This distinction is, as noted, the common legal practice today; causing a miscarriage is not regarded as homicide.

The best conclusion one might make from biblical citation is from Ecclesiastes: "As you do not know how the Spirit comes to the bones in the womb of the mother with child, so you do not know the work of God who makes everything" (Ecclesiastes 11:5). The ultimate problem with all the above citations is that they misread the Bible as a direct moral treatise rather than as a story of Creation and Salvation—an argument I shall take up in the next chapter. There are moral implications and obligations derived from the Creation-Salvation story, but they are more complex than the presumed anti-abortion citations would suggest.

A Good Word About "Soul"

In earlier discussions of abortion, Catholic moralists did not use the notion of "person" as the governing category. The moral argument turned on the notion of the "soul." St. Thomas Aquinas distinguished the fault of abortion before and after "ensoulment." This argument is not usually offered today because en*soul*ment suggests some special theological concern that does not work in a secular argument. It is worth a brief comment, however, on ensoulment in the quite specific secular meaning to which Aquinas appealed.

The notion of soul in Thomas's philosophy was derived from Aristotle and his treatise *Peri Psyche* in Greek. *Peri Psyche*, from which we obviously get "psychology," was not quite what we would think. The book is not just about the mind, emotions, and all that—the modern notion of "higher function"—it is about the human body and its assemblage of hierarchically ordered biological functions. Some bodily functions are "vegetative" (for example, digestion), others are "animal" (the ability to move about in the environment), and some are "rational." There is a complex interplay between these differing biological processes. No food for my vegetative functions and my rational functions are disoriented. Anxiety upsets my stomach. The most interesting point about Thomas's view is that all living things have a "soul." There is a vegetative soul, an animal soul, and a rational soul. This sounds strange and theological to modern ears, but the claim is quite sensible and essential to understanding Aquinas on abortion and, by extension, how one might assess the moral standing of the fetus.

The Latin translation of *Peri Psyche* is helpful. *De Anima,* as it is usually translated, could well be translated into English as "On Animation" or "On Living." An ensouled item is something that is living. A growing tomato is a living tomato; when it is plucked it ceases its vegetative life—it loses its tomato soul. A living dog and a dead dog are obviously very different. The soul of a tomato or a dog is not some mysterious power within. It is nothing more than the living thing doing its thing: living. Aristotle and Thomas thought it most important to make this subtle point because the biological structure of a living thing remains the same living or dead. In the case of the dead, the machinery doesn't happen to be operating. Aristotle has a telling analogy. If the whole body were the eye, then seeing would be the soul of the eye. Seeing is the eye "doing its thing." There is no reason why a blind researcher could not understand fully the biological mechanism of the eye. The researcher would know *how* the eye works, but he would not know "seeing": what the working-living eye actually does.

What is the relevance of all this biological metaphysics to the modern abortion debate? For Aristotle and Aquinas you do not have a *human* being, *human* ensoulment, or a "person" until you have a functioning *human* body. The fetus goes through "vegetative" and "animal" stages with appropriate vegetable and animal souls, but it needs a human body to function as a human and have a human soul. Aquinas's view that abortion before the quickening is different was based on his notion of *human* ensoulment—that is, when the fetal body becomes a human body. Deliberate abortions or spontaneous miscarriages of the early fetus could not constitute the death of a human being because a "human body-soul" had not yet been developed. Aquinas certainly knew that, left alone, the early fetus might well develop a proper body, a human soul, but the death of the early fetus could not be regarded as the death of a human being. Like Augustine, Aquinas regarded abortion before viability as contraceptive and thus immoral. Neither Augustine nor Aquinas would agree with the present prevailing rhetoric of abortion as "murder." For these two great theologians, only if one considered contraception equivalent to murder would the current rhetoric be appropriate. It may be unfortunate and regretted, and, if by abortion, would need moral justification, but the act would not constitute murder.

However antique one may regard all this talk about "soul," Aquinas and Aristotle are basically correct. The issue in the abortion debate is not about the killing of a human being or person but a *potential* human being. It is important to state the issue accurately. Before the distinction is lightly dismissed, it explains why we do not react to early miscarriage as a major health problem. It explains why the Church does not baptize in vitro embryos or hold funerals for miscarried fetuses. It may seem overly literal and precise, but for Aquinas one could not say that the death of the fetus before quickening is "murder." There is just no human soul to be murdered. We may have serious moral responsibilities to the early fetus—I think that we do—but should the fetus die through miscarriage or induced abortion, one cannot escalate the death to the level of homicide (there is not yet a *homo*).

One of the common factors in assessing the legitimacy of an abortion is whether there is a presumption in favor of *actual* life, the life of the mother, over the *potential* life of the fetus. For Orthodox Judaism, the presumption is for the actual life of the mother. In Catholic morality the presumption is for potential life, the fetus; abortion of a potential person is not permitted to save the life of an actual person, the pregnant woman. One of the most doubtful parts of the pro-life criticism of abortion is the elimination of the distinction between the fetus (a potential person) and a newborn or the mother (actual persons). In pro-life rhetoric there is no distinction between "unborn" and "newborn," as if we were talking about the very same entity but in two different places. While the biology is not the same as the preformationists', the sense is the same: the fetus is a fully realized human being or person from conception. The older biology actually fits the pro-life argument—the fetus was only *quantitatively* different from the newborn; it just gets bigger over time. In modern biology, the process involves *qualitative* bodily change. Aquinas's theory, the Church's sacramental practice, and common sense regard the moral status of the fetus differently according to the *qualitatively* different stages of development. In common law and much common opinion, the actual woman has greater moral weight than the potential—sometimes *very* potential—fetal "person."

Conclusion?

Is the fetus a person? I don't think that there is a once and for all categorical answer. It is clear enough that a "naturalistic" description whether "human embryo" or "high functioning" is not decisive for moral assessment. No natural description determines a moral category as such. "Person" is used in pro-life arguments as a moral term through and through. If you believe that abortion is an intrinsic evil, you may well be led to invest the fetus with a moral status (person) appropriate to the moral judgment. There is a problem, however, with moving from "abortion is an intrinsic evil" to "the fetus is a person." It requires an overwrought reading of "intrinsic evil."

There are intrinsic evils and intrinsic evils. Sometimes it is permissible and even morally necessary to commit an intrinsic evil. It is not only permissible to lie to the Gestapo, it is a moral duty. One commits an intrinsic evil for which there is an overriding moral excuse. (Catholic casuists have argued from time to time that lying

es that the other de-
bortion in an ectopic
nore honest to call a
rtion as an abortion.
sreads "intrinsic evil"
hat intrinsic evil is al-
vity for which we can
nvest the fetus with a
ation. The fetus is re-
he fetus is an innocent
n self-defense, war, or

ocent person is, in my
inability to construct
n innocent person has
ractical wisdom. Prac-
hing of intrinsic goods
o answer that question
her evils—some more
ods of various weight.
ude that the abortion
e woman whose life is
ntinue to nurture her
clude that the decision
vas thoughtless, it was
unish a spouse, and so
used is not to say that
uch. The woman who
with the intrinsic evil
How serious the moral
beliefs and the circum-
seriously immoral that
ce, forbidding abortion
ertain.

The Church's position on abortion constitutes a failure of practical wisdom. Eliding "intrinsic evil" with "inexcusable evil" leads to assigning "person" to the fetus. It accounts for the overwrought rhetoric that has marked the public statements of the bishops quoted at the beginning of the book. My best conclusion: one cannot label the fetus a person. While the fetus deserves great respect, it cannot be at the expense of devastating someone who is unequivocally a person—the pregnant person.

Pregnant Persons

Stages on Life's Way

I have argued that "person" by itself is too thin a concept to specify the exact range of our moral duties; one has to consider specific persons. We determine our moral duties in terms of a host of factors that qualify the person and our attendant duty. Biological status is one important factor. Age is a biological fact about humans, but how aged persons are regarded by themselves and in their culture can be strikingly varied for good or ill. The aged may be revered for wisdom or sent off to play shuffleboard in Sun City. Pregnancy as a biological condition also sets a moral framework. What is the moral situation of a woman as this may be qualified by age and situation? Pregnancy carries a different human meaning for an abandoned underage girl and a happily married woman. Health, economic circumstances, relationships, and a host of other topics are likely to be added into what it means for *this* woman to be pregnant.

Traditional Catholic natural law theory seems to interpret pregnancy solely from biology. The title of John Paul's "theology of the body" talks, *Man and Woman Created He Them,* suggests concentration on biological difference as determinative for duty. A pregnant woman is in a particular biological state and it is from this state alone that her moral duty is to be specified. The problem is that biological male and biological female are only sketches for being a man or a woman. Gertrude Stein was famous for proclaiming "a rose, is a rose, is a rose." That is an appropriate characterization for natural entities like roses and rocks—they are just what they are, roses or rocks. It is not clear that human persons can be defined by iterations of biological sameness. If I may resort to fancy philosophy, I think those philosophers are correct who intone, "Human being is that being whose being is in question." Unlike the rose that is a rose, I am everlastingly asking "Who am I?" A woman is not a woman is not a woman when it comes to who she is. A pregnant woman is not just her biological pregnancy, a clear biological state—she is *this* pregnant person in some stage of her life and times with whatever happy expectations or dread that state may hold.

A pregnant woman finds herself not merely in a biological condition, but also defined within a particular set of cultural, economic, social, moral, and so forth circumstances. The move from biological condition to *this* pregnant person in her specific setting is crucial in moral deliberation about abortion. Both pro-choice and pro-life advocates have a tendency to abstract from the specific condition of *this* pregnancy as a spiritual event in the life of the woman. Pro-life concentrates on biological sameness, while pro-choice bypasses the moral and spiritual overtones by valuing choice, not what is chosen. How does *this* woman at *this* age and circumstance in *this* culture understand and evaluate her pregnant state? How *should* she evaluate these various factors? Pregnancy is more than a biological process—it is a spiritual life event.

The Container View

In an extensive and detailed defense of the pro-life position, philosopher and Catholic convert Francis J. Beckwith repeatedly argues the case that there is no moral difference between a fetus in the womb and a newborn because "geographical location" does not change a person's moral status. Whatever the exact characterization of the relation between a woman and the fetus in her womb, "geographical" hardly seems the proper designation. To a spectator the womb may just be a different location, but the pregnant woman is not an observer of pregnancy; she is a full-scale biological and psychological participant. Her womb is not just one place around the house to park the fetus. One critic calls the "geographical" claim the "container view" of pregnancy. The container view of pregnancy fits well with pre-formationist embryology, either in its earlier guise or in the modern notion that there is a full moral person from the moment of conception. The woman is ultimately regarded as the fetus's passive nurturer, container, or "environment." Old and new pre-formationism casts the women as a minor actor in the pregnancy drama, a sort of hired nursemaid.

Recognizing the shift from spectator to participant, from passive nurturer to essential actor, is crucial in evaluating and understanding pregnancy and abortion. "Pregnant woman" fits the medical text and a spectator's abstraction, but it fails to grasp the lived reality of a particular woman's pregnancy experience. For the woman, pregnancy is *her* lived experience; she is participating in her pregnancy with whatever richness and poverty of spirit she possesses. The passive, container view of pregnancy diminishes the woman to a biological function, and not even accurate biology.

It is not easy to describe the lived experience of pregnancy. After all, half the human race—the half in which this author is located—never has the experience. If one turns to the testimony of women themselves, it would be impossible to locate some single universal experience of pregnancy. Obviously women experience pregnancy in many different ways, from exhilarating to exhausting, a time of hope or the last moment of despair. Examples of women's experience of pregnancy would not only contain many varied accounts, but there is also the problem noted earlier in Henry James's comments about "experience." Lots of people manage to drift through life, even pregnancy, without ever *experiencing* the very moments in which they participate. Maybe some women do experience their pregnancy as "containers." I think that they miss the meaning of pregnancy in their lives. A woman who experiences her pregnancy as a unique joy or a devastating tragedy inserts her person into the biological process; she is not just the passive recipient of a bodily change. Human persons should not and probably cannot experience biological events passively, whether these events are adolescence, old age, or pregnancy.

The container view seems mistaken even from a biological standpoint. In contrast to pre-formationist embryology, in which the woman does seem to be properly a passive container, we now know that the woman's whole physiology is mobilized in the formation of fetal life. From gross anatomy to subtle hormonal changes, the experience of her body is altered. Striking bodily changes can and usually do produce manifest changes in self-image. Sylvia Plath, considering her pregnant body, said she had become "a riddle in nine syllables." The biological reality of pregnancy is directly reflected in the way we describe the relation between the woman and her fetus. Far from merely feeding something already "pre-formed," the fetus is bone of *her* bone, flesh of *her* flesh; the child-to-be is *hers* in a stronger sense than that of a passive nurturer. Judith Thompson's violinist example, useful as it is, abstracts from the intimate relation of the pregnant woman and her fetus. The child in the womb is not the violinist in the next bed over feeding off my kidneys. Even if I give my kidney to my ailing sister, I do not thereby establish the intimacy of blood and bone that pregnancy entails.

The experience of pregnancy for the woman rests in a uniquely intimate relation of self-and-other. The fetus is an "other" but also "flesh of her flesh." The French feminist philosopher Julia Kristeva offers a striking account of pregnancy in an extraordinary essay with the provocative title *Stabat Mater*, the title of the traditional hymn about Mary standing by the Cross. Kristeva says that pregnancy for the woman's consciousness is a kind of schizophrenia: the woman senses that she is both herself and yet another. To convey in her essay the paradoxical and extraordinary sense of the pregnant state, the text of Kristeva's essay contains blocks of bold type expressing the mother's emotional cries and feelings. The bold-faced passages of passion are embedded in her prose text as the fetus is embedded in the ordinary life of the mother. Visually and logically the poetic outcries don't seem to belong, but there they boldly are, pulling the reader's eye and sense away from straightforward prose. For Kristeva, pregnancy is like this split-but-single text. As the woman is herself-and-another, her essay is both straight philosophy (over which she has control) and something else that cannot be separated out (about which she can cry out). The child is the woman, *her* flesh, though it becomes other. Kristeva expresses the poignancy of pregnancy and birth:

> One does not give birth in pain, one gives birth to pain: the child represents it and henceforth it settles in, it is continuous. Obviously you may close your eyes, cover up your ears, teach courses, run errands, tidy the house, think of objects, subjects. But a mother is always branded by pain, she yields to it. "And a sword will pierce your own soul too."

In a critique of Judith Thompson's tale of the violinist, critic John Wilcox complained that the example is "weird." When has anything like that actually happened? In contrast, he points out that pregnancy is a common, ordinary phenomenon. Common maybe, but ordinary it is not. Pregnancy is not "weird" in the manner of Thompson's bizarre story but, if Plath's wonder at her riddling pregnant self or Kristeva's "schizophrenia" are even partially correct, pregnancy can be as disruptive as mental derangement. Puberty is another biological change that disrupts self-possession. The simple self of the child is possessed by the "demons" of hormonal drives and gross bodily change. Finding an assured self while possessed by great bodily change is no easy matter. Kristeva sees a mother's relation to the child as permanently disruptive of the orderly self who "tidies up the house." Not the self-contained self and body, "A mother is a continuous separation, a division of the very flesh."

The pregnant woman's tie to the *other* is more than warm social metaphor; it is based on an intimacy of blood and bone with an *other*. This pregnancy paradox of self-and-other underlines what is defective about casting the abortion debate in terms of "rights," the clash between the fetus's right to life and the woman's right to choose. Rights make sense when there are two clearly different entities, me and you. The trouble with pregnancy is that there is no clear "me" (pregnant woman here) and "you" (fetus over there). That works if the womb is a container, but it doesn't work for the other who is "flesh of my flesh."

Intimacy and the Abortion Debate

Recognition of the unique self-and-other experience of pregnancy cuts both ways in the abortion debate. Against the pro-choice side it emphasizes that the decision to abort is not a simple decision about some "external" other. Ridding herself of her fetus is not simply ignoring a bad companion, divorcing a husband, or unplugging a dependent violinist. Pregnancy carried to term or ending in abortion relates to the deepest sense of the woman herself: Who am I after all? Through pregnancy? After abortion? After motherhood? One of the reasons that surrogate motherhood is so problematic is that the surrogate is often reluctant to surrender *her* child to another. If surrogacy were to become routine practice, it would be because surrogates regard themselves as nurturing containers with no deep bond to the child of their pregnancy. It is hard to imagine this view of pregnancy as a social good. Carrying a child to term, aborting, offering to be a surrogate, or putting a child up for adoption creates or severs a relationship that is more intimate and unbreakable than any other relation one may have to another human being. You can divorce a spouse—you can't divorce a child. To be sure, not every woman may self-consciously experience this intimate bond, yet it is hard to believe that the ties do not remain deep in her sense of self. Insofar as pro-choice slights the intimacy of the relationship, and how the decision of abortion reflects back into the self of the woman, the argument is faulty to the biological reality that underlies the deep experience of pregnancy. In considering abortion a woman *ought*, morally ought, to consider what it means to refuse or break such an intimate bond. The African American poet Gwendolyn Brooks gets the moral point correctly in her famous poem "The Mother": "Abortion will not let you forget./You remember the children that you got and that you did not get."

But if pro-choice isolates the woman from her fetus, pro-life isolates the fetus from the woman. The limitation of pro-life can be illustrated by assuming a situation in which the government required abortions for reasons of population control. Pro-life would obviously find such a legal mandate abhorrent. Why? Because of the death of the fetus. That seems to be a truncated moral assessment of the situation. At least part of the moral fault in such legislation would be diminishment of the woman. She would be viewed as a morally inconsequential container of a socially undesirable product. Her self, her choice, and her desire to have a baby would be denied value. Her unique capacity as a woman would be blocked. (Pro-choice would, of course, find required abortion abhorrent precisely because it disregarded the woman's choice.)

If the woman is brought back into the picture such that her needs and wishes count, the moral argument against abortion cannot rest solely on the fate of the fetus. The woman's health, her commitments and responsibilities, and her psychological state become factors in assessing her pregnancy. Becoming pregnant or refusing pregnancy, carrying a child to term or seeking an abortion, relate to deep experiences for a woman, experiences that involve her full biological reality, even the possibility of her death, as well as a psychological and spiritual experience of her whole person. The satisfaction unto joy of birth or the regret unto tragedy of abortion occur as profound spiritual moments for the woman.

The fact that pregnancy and abortion present profound issues for how the woman defines herself, her moral *persona*, suggests why there is sympathy for abortion in the case of underage women or for abortion after rape or incest. The nature of the fetus is the same whatever the age of the woman or the circumstances of the pregnancy. Construct the situation as a contest of rights between separate parties and no solution seems obvious. But, if pregnancy focuses on the pregnant person, the adolescent person may be so fragile that her psychic life can be permanently shattered by pregnancy. The challenge to the self of the rape victim is already severe; early abortion will not necessarily erase the threat to the self, but forcing her to carry the child to term may be the final destruction of her spirit.

Consideration of the special state of pregnancy and its intimate connection to the individual *persona* of the woman explains why categorical moral assessment of abortion is so difficult. There is a heavy valence toward "choice" because of the centrality of the individual pregnant person. Her decision about abortion is, or should be, a defining moment for her life. The woman's decision for or against abortion is a decision about who she is and will be as *this* person: one who can carry a child or seek an abortion in the particular situation of her life.

If it is essential in the moral assessment of abortion to consider the circumstances of the woman, not the least of the circumstances is the fetal life she carries. It is the fact of fetal life, after all, that is forcing a decision. An acquaintance of mine is a physician at a large university health clinic; she is an ardent pro-choice advocate. She did, however, acknowledge serious reservations about a young woman who opined that this abortion, her third, was "the nicest abortion she had ever had." Believing as I do that abortion is an "intrinsic evil," the sort of procedure one would accept only to remedy a worse situation, I agree with the physician: no abortion can be "nice." Anyone who holds that view suffers from serious moral blindness. The decision to abort must—morally must—involve weighing the status of fetal life against factors sufficiently compelling to justify the action. There must be a moral excuse for abortion. Sometimes the moral excuse seems so clear that it is difficult to see how one could assign blame to the woman's decision. I offer two cases in point.

Hard Cases

Years ago I was debating the issue of abortion with Joseph Fletcher, who was famous for creating what was called "situation ethics." I took a generally conservative view about abortion. Fletcher countered with a situation that I assume was true, though its factual truth is irrelevant to his argument. He said that in the Nazi concentration camps Jewish women who were pregnant were immediately sent to the gas chambers. In the camps, Jewish doctor inmates performed thousands of abortions on pregnant women to save their lives. He challenged my conservative stance. "What would you say to that?" I replied, "Joe, no one could possibly condemn a woman for having an abortion in that situation." According to official Catholic teaching, direct abortion, such as was practiced in this case, is always prohibited. Presumably, I was wrong to suggest otherwise.

Fletcher's case may have been fictional—though I suspect it was true—but a recent newspaper story described the case of an abortion performed on a nine-year-old Brazilian girl, pregnant with twins following repeated rape since the age of six by her stepfather. The local prelate, Archbishop José Cardoso Sobrinho, excommunicated the doctors and the girl's mother, but not the rapist. Rape, he said, was bad, but abortion was even worse. Although Brazilian law permits abortion, following standard Catholic moral teaching, the archbishop asserted, "The law of God is higher than any human law." The Brazilian government was shocked by the archbishop's action. Even the Vatican initially said that the archbishop's decision was hasty. Later, the Vatican's top bioethics official, Archbishop Rino Fischella, went further: "[The] credibility of our teaching took a blow as it appeared, in the eyes of many, to be insensitive, incomprehensible and lacking mercy." The apparent censure by Archbishop Fischella was appealed by priests from Cardoso's diocese, and, in a final judgment, the Congregation for the Doctrine of the Faith (CDF) ruled that Cardoso had acted "with every pastoral solicitude" and Archbishop Fischella had by no means qualified the Church's teaching on abortion. The controversy has continued: several members of the Pontifical Academy for Life, of which Fischella is the head, have circulated a letter calling for his reassignment because, so the letter states, "[he] does not understand what absolute respect for human lives entails."

It is said that hard cases make bad law. I pointed out to Fletcher that he was not a "situation ethicist" if he meant to imply that the concentration camp case offered blanket permission for all abortions. Nevertheless, hard cases point to limitations in the generalities with which law is necessarily framed. One may sweepingly condemn abortion but then, as many prohibitory laws indicate, make exceptions for hard cases like rape, incest, or the life of the mother. In the Brazilian case rape, incest, and the life of the mother were all factors, but they did not alter Archbishop Cardoso's judgment.

What is one to make of these two cases? My moral assessment in both cases is that condemnation of the abortion was mistaken. I would conjecture that a great many people would agree and that no jury in law would be likely to convict the concentration camp doctors or the Brazilian physicians of a crime. The Brazilian officials were closer to the proper moral assessment than Archbishop Cardoso. Obvious deep disagreement about such hard cases should, one would like to believe, give pause to Church condemnation. Archbishop Fischella's "insensitive, incomprehensible and lacking in mercy" seems closer to the moral sense of the situation than the later opinion of the CDF.

Archbishop Cardoso, the CDF, and official Catholic teaching are, in effect, treating abortion as "statutory": an offense in which the physical facts are not subject to qualification by circumstance. Statutory rape holds that sexual intercourse by an adult with a minor is criminal regardless of circumstance. Even if "consensual" the action is rape and punishable as such. Abortion as "statutory" ignores any and all circumstances. (Even the Catholic exceptions like "abortion" for an ectopic pregnancy are not regarded as *direct* abortion but a surgical intervention that only indirectly causes loss of the fetus.) Presumably an offense is regarded as statutory when the act is deemed so heinous that it is "inexcusable." There is no excuse in law for the rape of a minor, no excuse in Church law for an abortion.

Is abortion in all circumstances so heinous that it can never be excused? My sense of how the concentration camp case would be judged and the reaction of the Brazilian government suggest that many sane people regard abortion as excusable in such grave circumstances. The worry of Church officials seems to be that in dealing with the hard cases one will descend the infamous slippery slope. Admit this hard-case exception, then this case that is almost as difficult and so on until any pain or annoyance becomes an excuse for abortion. Best to have *no* exceptions. A "no-exceptions" stance is common to both pro-life and pro-choice advocates. Pro-life wants no exceptions to prohibition; pro-choice wants no exceptions to abortion on demand.

"No exceptions, no excuses" from either pro-life or pro-choice is morally flawed. In the case of the Catholic condemnation of all abortions, it is not clear that it is even consistent. Archbishop Fischella's view that Cardoso's action was "insensitive . . . and lacking in mercy" depended on consideration of the unusual circumstances of the case. When mercy is called for, it is intended to qualify or withdraw moral judgment. If mercy cannot be extended to the Jewish women in the concentration camp or the Brazilian child, it would seem to have no application. If mercy is applicable to the woman undergoing the abortion, it is difficult to see how one can punish the one who provides the abortion. If it was a mercy for the girl to have the abortion in the first place, it was merciful of the doctors to offer their services.

It is not only Archbishop Fischella's initial reaction that seems to contradict Church policy; official Church law itself presents a problem for the stance of "no excuses." Not all bishops agreed with Archbishop Cardoso. A few argued that excommunication was inappropriate based on clause 1324 in canon law: "The penalty prescribed in the law . . . must be diminished if . . . one has been compelled by grave fear." It is certainly plausible to argue that the concentration camp example involved "grave fear." How about the

Brazilian case? One Brazilian doctor said that an appropriate caesarian section could have safely delivered the twins and noted that this operation had been performed on other very young birth mothers. All well and good. What about the grave fear of a nine-year-old about having to carry a pregnancy to term following rape from the age of six?

The question to ask about Canon 1324 is what "diminishment" means. I have agreed with the Catholic position that abortion is an "intrinsic evil," so there is something is wrong about abortion even in the hard cases. Nevertheless, one may have a legitimate excuse for the wrong that has been committed. "Diminishment" is not the same as "dismissal" of any fault line—that is why one must offer an excuse commensurate with the seriousness of the situation. If the excuse is adequate there is no condemnation. If the excuse fails, then "punishment" is proper. If it succeeds, one is left with the "punishment" of regret and the obligation to avoid, if possible, any similar dilemma. The young woman who blithely accepted her third abortion as "nice" was a moral failure because she thought that abortion required no moral excuse.

The apparent exception in Canon 1324 should be a factor for Church policy, even though admitting circumstance makes it difficult to draw the line between what may be excusable and what is not. How much "fear" is "grave fear"? What are the proper objects of fear? The fragile health of the mother? Dire economic distress? Fear of social disgrace? Loss of job opportunities? And so on through all the worries and concerns that can be posed by pregnancy.

In moral and legal assessment it can be quite difficult to draw the line. Fear of the slippery slope can make absolute, statutory condemnation attractive, but the price of clarity is too high. Of course, one *can* slide down a slippery slope into mere subjectivism, but the function of practical wisdom is to perceive the range of interpretation allowable. As stated, practical wisdom is an art derived from practice and experience, it is difficult to obtain and rare, but it is the final and essential arbiter of morality. Practical wisdom can sort out motives and circumstance as best one can for the abortion and then make a *moral* judgment. The *law*, in contrast, is not as suited for evaluating complex circumstance and the intimate psychological state of the woman. If one considers abortion restrictions in other countries, they make the usual exceptions for rape, incest, and the life of the mother, but they usually have a broad exception dealing with the mental health of the woman. Anti-abortion advocates are very resistant to any mental health exceptions because of their breadth and vagueness. But there are real mental health issues like "grave fear" that seem to "diminish penalty." Ultimately it is the woman herself who suffers the grave fear even if it seems to be for less than grave reasons. Perhaps she can be counseled to deal with her fear. The law can require prior counseling, but in the long run the law is not capable of judging that the woman's fears are genuine or inappropriate. She is, for her moral good or ill, the ultimate judge. Pro-choice is the sensible *legal* solution.

Chapter Five

Church Morality

Much of the previous chapter's argument that abortion must be evaluated in the light of the circumstances of the woman will be recapitulated in this chapter, with one significant difference. I want to look now at *Christian* or *Church* morality as something different than the sort of rational or commonsense arguments that I have used so far. *Church* morality is not necessarily different in content, but it grounds morality in a religious story. It is that story, the biblical story—for Christians, the story of Jesus—that creates an ultimate framework for morals. How are we to act in a Creator's world? This is a question that day-to-day morality seldom asks. If, however, the question is posed as it is in the biblical story, there are ultimate considerations that affect the assessment of abortion.

If you were to read my local diocesan newspaper—and it is not atypical—you would think that anti-abortion is the heart and center of Christian witness. The major media sources are not deceived when they see the Catholic Church through the lens of the hot-button issues of abortion, gay marriage, and the like. These are the obsessive topics of leading Catholic spokespersons and pamphleteers. Anti-abortion is "foundational"; any other stance is inexcusable. While I think that this is an ill-considered moral assessment of abortion, it is even worse as the foundation stone of Christianity and Church.

Equating abortion and "culture of death" fails to locate authentic Christian preaching about life and death. Christianity stands over and against the lure of dark and lovely death, but demonizing abortion distracts from the true biblical message. To the extent that abortion is a Christian issue—and I think it should be—it is based on a different set of spiritual assumptions than those of the standard pro-life campaign. Positioning anti-abortion as foundational, subject to absolutist moral condemnation, distorts the meaning of Christ and the meaning of the Church. It obfuscates the true meaning of Christianity as "the culture of life."

There is nothing perverse about the Church teaching morality, but moral teaching is not the essence of the Church. There are many outside the Roman Catholic Church or any Christian community who are opposed to abortion for moral or political reasons. The Church's overall position on abortion is—or should be—different, because the reality of "church" frames the question. Church moral teaching exists within a larger understanding than direct moral argument. Encapsulating morality in the idea of the Church is ultimately derived from the Bible. Whatever the "moral" teaching of the Church might be, it is, in the final analysis, a function of how to read Scripture. Christian morality is not, in short, a "stand-alone" moral position.

When Catholic commentators present their anti-abortion case as a simple derivation from moral law, they obscure the Gospel message, which is always more than a moral philosophy. This might not be so bad—we can use all the moral arguments we can get—but confusing the straight moral argument on abortion and a Church teaching distorts the meaning of church to the point that the existence of a "church" is no longer necessary. To avoid this distortion, I want to round out this critique by discussing the idea of "church."

An adequate understanding of "church" would ultimately require the lengthiest of treatises on theology, the Bible, Christology, sacramentalism, and so on. All that is beyond the scope of this book. What is presented is a sketch of a sketch. I believe it discusses essential issues, but I am under no illusion that it is even close to the last word. Nevertheless, since I believe that the Church is pursuing the wrong crusade in its adamant and "foundational" opposition to abortion, I am compelled to say what I can. This chapter is necessary in rounding off the argument for Catholic believers, since they may well judge that whatever the limitations of a straight moral argument against abortion, the moral dictates of Christianity trump mere philosophy. While a secular reader may not be initially interested in what seems an internal church question, I would suggest that everyone has an "ultimate worldview"—a "religion" in that sense—that colors everyday morality. Morality is a higher venture than one might rationally suppose and the biblical view is hardly to be discounted.

Volunteers or Conscripts

What is a church? In American law, a church, the Catholic Church included, is classified as a "voluntary organization." A church is an organization that people choose to join because they agree with its moral, political, or social agenda. For the law, a church is an organization like the National Rifle Association (NRA) or the Pro-Choice America: a gathering of volunteers advocating a cause. Despite the legal designation, the Catholic Church—and this is true of all Christian churches—is not in its own *inner* meaning a voluntary organization. Strictly speaking, the Church is an *in*voluntary society. The Church is *in*voluntary in the sense that the class of Nazi Holocaust survivors is involuntary. One does not choose to join the group of Holocaust survivors—the group comes into being because *something happened* to just those people.

Like Holocaust survivors, people come to regard themselves as Christians because they believe that something has happened to them through the life and action of Jesus Christ. Holocaust victims were condemned to death by the Nazis; Christians are saved from death by Jesus. Philosopher Iris Murdoch got it right when she commented that in religion we are not volunteers—we are conscripts. Something has happened (racial condemnation, salvation) that creates a special community.

The common claim that one needs grace, the "gift" of faith, in order to be Christian expresses the fact that we don't choose Christianity—we are given a relation to God and faith; we are chosen.

Christians claim to be a "chosen people" no less than the ancient Israelites. The Israelites could have said "no" when God chose them as his people, but they did not and could not have initiated divine favor. The fact that being Christian is *in*voluntary (it happens to *you*, *you* have been chosen) does not, of course, mean that one necessarily attends services on Sunday. Not everyone who survived the Holocaust will be active in the drive for a Holocaust memorial. One may even actively resist being conscripted by history. I choose not to be chosen. A Holocaust survivor may do everything she can to put the Holocaust and its memory out of her life and thought. It is a grief too great to bear. Being chosen by God is not necessarily a key to ordinary happiness and good fortune—witness the prophets, the life of Jesus, and the many saints and martyrs. Like Jonah, I would just as soon not go to Nineveh.

The most common example of an *in*voluntary society is the family. We do not choose our father and mother, and no voluntary society to which we later *choose* to belong is likely to have a more profound effect on our life and values than our family. I can, of course, reject my family, make a flamboyant denial of my parents, and write a blistering denunciation of "Mommy Dearest." Perhaps I drag myself sullenly through holiday gatherings. Maybe I just run away but feel cheated out of the happy upbringing of others. And so on. In any of those modes my family has determined me in a life of rejection. Like it or not, family is forever.

With the examples of Holocaust and family at hand, one can begin to grasp the inner nature of the Church. People belong to Church because they believe that something happened to them because of the life of Jesus of Nazareth. What can that possibly mean? What could have happened in the life of a rather obscure prophet in a faraway corner of an ancient empire that could provide the spiritual setting for my life? I might believe that when Caesar crossed the Rubicon he initiated a long chain of political events that are still playing out in my life even today, but the life and death of an itinerant Nazarene preacher! What did this Jesus person do? To state the matter simply, but in quite orthodox language, the life of this Jesus incorporated humanity into God's family. As we are "stuck" with the family into which we are born, because of Jesus we are "stuck" as brothers and sisters in God's family. Because of Jesus, the history of human war and destruction is not a clash of strangers but a case of sibling rivalry.

There is much interpretation needed to open up the Christian claim. Are only some people touched by Jesus' action or is everybody saved? (I think it has to be everybody, though some will refuse salvation for complex reasons.) And what exactly is "salvation" anyhow? However one deals with these complex theological issues, the critical point for my purpose is the *in*voluntary nature of being Christian. Because the Church is an involuntary organization, the "morality" of the members is not something they enter into from a position of historical neutrality. In Church morality we do not start as unencumbered agents "rationally" deciding to join a cause. A Holocaust survivor does not make up a spiritual life freely; it is already determined by a tragic history. In a recent novel, Elie Wiesel, himself a concentration camp victim, depicts a Holocaust survivor saying to himself, "Why, when I close my eyes, do I always have the feeling of being in hostile territory?" A "morality" for hostile territory is not the same as for a one that has been redeemed. Christians claim that they live in a "redeemed" world, and this is meant to shape their actions. The distinguished Catholic moral theologian Charles Curran speaks about the "stance" of the Catholic moralist, the fact that the Catholic moral theologian speaks from *within* a history of Creation, Covenant, Incarnation, Redemption, and Judgment.

Teacher of Faith and Morals

The Church claims to be "a teacher of faith and morals." It is a claim that demands interpretation. Part of the problem depends on the meaning of "and." Is the Church a teacher of two separate subjects, like a high-school teacher who instructs in algebra and Spanish, or is there some inner relation between "faith" and "morals"? Agreeing with Charles Curran that Catholic morality begins from a special stance, I would argue that whatever morals may be preached by the Church, they are *derived from faith*—from the historical stance in which we find ourselves. In a secular context, being saved from death or disaster by someone should certainly affect my stance toward my own life and that of my rescuer. If I ignore that "salvation," my actions will be judged in the light of that fact. If I blandly toss off the fact that my life was saved and snub the rescuer, I will be faulted for ingratitude. In a fundamental sense, Christian morality is a morality of gratitude.

The other term that needs interpretation in the claim to teach faith and morals is the sense in which the Church "teaches," the sense in which Jesus is a "teacher." It is a common characterization of Jesus that he is a great *teacher*. In the New Testament, people often address him as "teacher." Because Jesus is a teacher, so the Christian churches claim that they teach what he taught. In the Catholic Church, teaching is emphasized, with moral teaching out in front. Catholics are enjoined to obey the Roman *magisterium* (the word comes from *magister*, the Latin for "teacher") as the final arbiter of Church teaching on faith and morals. The pope can even teach infallibly under proper conditions. While anti-abortion has not been made an infallible teaching, it certainly has taken on that air.

Despite the common view that the Church teaches, there are significant problems about *Church* teaching. When the papal encyclical *Mater et Magister* (Mother and Teacher) was issued, criticizing capitalist economies, a group of economically conservative Catholics led by William F. Buckley objected. Somewhere in the heat of battle the slogan "Mater, Si, Magister, No" came to express their counterposition. The Church may be *Mother* Church, but not *Teacher* Church. Much as I disagree with such conservative economic views, the slogan was half-right. There is something odd about the Church as "teacher." What is basic to Church membership is not following some teachings, but having a certain "mother," living in our Father's "family." Mothers and fathers do "teach," but their "teaching" is deeper than encyclicals. Parents may offer the soundest moral counsel, but subvert the teaching by their tone and actions. Parents may offer wretched moral views, but happily contradict them in their manifest behavior. What we "learn" from our parents, what they "teach," is the shape of our person. Angry parents may convey sound moral lessons but produce angry children—a more fundamental lesson learned than a correct moral catechism. It is the person of parents, not their moral philosophy, that is the fundamental lesson. We are taught in and through the person of parents who we are as persons. If that lesson is defective, it is far from easy to remedy.

It is crucial in evaluating the Church's "teaching" on abortion to recognize that the Church is not, then, a moral teacher in the ordinary sense. There are great moral teachers. Plato was a great moral teacher. Jesus offered many moral teachings, but they were basically the Torah teaching of the great rabbis. For orthodox Christianity, Jesus offers something beyond teaching. The distinguished Jewish scholar Jacob Neusner some years ago wrote a fascinating book, *A Rabbi Talks with Jesus* (the work most commented on in Benedict XVI's recent *Jesus of Nazareth*). Neusner's rabbi hears Jesus' Sermon on the Mount; he is impressed but troubled. In the evening he discuses his concerns with a fellow rabbi. "What did he leave out of Torah teaching?" asks the rabbi. Neusner's rabbi answers, "Nothing." "What did he add?" Answer: "Himself." Neusner's rabbi heard well. Jesus does say, "He who believes in *me* will never see death"—"*I* am the way, and the truth, and the life." A faculty member who proclaimed to his students "*I* am the truth" would never see tenure. The difference between Jesus and Plato or Hillel is that the latter wanted people to follow their *teachings*, not to be attached to their persons. Great teachers disappear behind their teachings. This is just what Jesus evidently did not do. There are students of Plato—he did, after all, found the first "university," the *academia*—and there is the School of Hillel, but there are followers of Jesus' person (the Church). To be a Christian is somehow to be linked to the *person* of Jesus. If the central issue of my life is "Who am I; what sort of person should I become?," Christians are shaped not by moral maxims, but by living in Christ. More than a "teacher," Jesus is "brother," his Father is "our Father." It is in the mystery of personal communion in God's family that we become Christian persons. All Church moral "teaching" is family teaching, the formation of the Christian persona.

A comment on "our *Father*." My earlier book, *Finding the Voice of the Church*, was sharply criticized as patriarchal by the outstanding feminist theologian Elizabeth Johnson, author of the groundbreaking *She Who Is*. In that book I did talk a lot about "Father" God while attempting to avoid despotic patriarchy. One hopes that our *Father* is like the father in the parable of the Prodigal Son, not the tyrant of family politics. There is no question but that all this "father" talk from God down to the parish priest can be dangerously distorting. The problem is finding some linguistic route around "father." Apparent solutions have their own problems. To talk of God as "parent" may be accurate, but lacks the personal resonance of "father" or "mother." Talk about God the Mother can appear to leave my half of the human race to the side, just as God the Father seems to exclude women. I finally choose to opt for the actual biblical language. In so doing, I agree with the late, great Catholic biblical scholar, Raymond E. Brown. He thought we should translate the Bible straight—and then point out that the language is misleading. Changing the texts to conform to present sensibilities creates the false impression that the Bible always states things just right, when in fact it is often in need of significant reinterpretation. I will stick to "our Father" despite the risk.

The *personal story* of Jesus is the important part of the New Testament. It is in his story that he is the savior and center of Christian worship. One can appreciate the centrality of story by considering current enthusiasm for the noncanonical Gospel of Thomas. The Gospel of Thomas consists of a string of Jesus' moral and spiritual comments—several of which are also found in the canonical Gospels. What is *not* in the Gospel of Thomas is the cross, death, and resurrection. Whatever the message of the Gospel of Thomas, it is in the sayings, not in the one who said them. The fact that Jesus, like Rabbi Akiba, led a saintly life and died a heroic death may lend an emotional attraction to the teaching, but finally it is the teaching that counts. Orthodoxy has it right: it is not his teachings that save—it is his person, his life and death, that saves. Jesus is not honored just as a great moral teacher; Christians proclaim him as a "savior." Barbara Brown Taylor comments that when Mary Magdalene addresses the Risen One as "teacher," she is rebuffed. Jesus says, "Do not hold on to me." One of the things we are not to hold on to is "teacher." As Taylor comments, "Teacher" was his Good Friday name; Easter Sunday he is "Savior."

What Jesus "saves" is our family tie to God, his Father and our Father. In the liturgy of Eucharist, which Catholics consider the heart of faith, believers partake of Jesus' body and blood, realizing a "blood relation" with Jesus that assures our spiritual family tie. The Eucharist is deeper lesson than even the best moral principle.

Bible as Story

I will have more to say about God's family and Jesus' saving that family tie, but I want to reinforce the claim that it is Jesus' life and death *story* that counts. This requires deciding how to read the Bible. What sort of book is it? Despite popular preaching, the Bible is not basically a book of moral teachings; it is a story—and the folks in the story are often anything but moral exemplars. The fact that the Bible is a story seems clear on its face as it traces the stories of Adam and Eve, the patriarchs, the Exodus, the history of the Jewish people, and the story of Jesus. One could, I suppose, consider the stories of the Bible like Aesop's fables: little allegories about morality. If nothing else, it would quite destroy the literary power of Scripture. We could reduce the book to a list of the moral lessons and forget about the illustrative stories. The whole thing would read like the Gospel of Thomas. St. Paul gets it right: "We preach Christ crucified" (1 Corinthians 1:23).

If Christians need a proof text *from* the Bible on *how to read* the Bible, they can turn to the Emmaus story in the Gospel of Luke. Two of the disciples are on the road out of Jerusalem after the disaster of Jesus' crucifixion. A stranger joins them and they recount to him the dispiriting events that have just taken place in Jerusalem. The stranger rebukes them for their despair over these events: "'Was it not necessary that the Messiah should suffer these things and enter into his glory?' Then beginning with Moses and all the prophets, he interpreted to them all the things about himself in all the scriptures" (Luke 24:26–27). The stranger, the risen Jesus, instructs the disciples to read the Bible as telling *his* story.

If one reads the Bible as a story, it is not just any old tale—it is a *family* story. The Bible starts with a parent God creating not singulars, but a "family," male and female. Unhappily, the first human family straightway acts to deny its parentage. They seek to "become like gods": self-creating without a "parental" relation. Once Adam and Eve reject common "parentage," they fall apart. When God asks Adam about eating the apple, he blames it on Eve. Out of Eden, the first family's sons introduce fratricide into the family story. Family persists as *the* biblical motif. God does not make a covenant with individuals, but with a family, the children of Abraham. The Bible story becomes the tale of that Jewish family. In the view of the great prophets, the children of Abraham keep forgetting their parent God, which leads to national disaster. Finally, God sends Jesus to recall us to God's family.

Jesus preaches "the reign of God." It is the same old story: the Romans, Jewish authorities, all of us through them, repeat the first sin, reject the message, and kill the preacher. At this point God might have sent another prophet hoping for better reception, or he might finally have decided to give up and let the human family self-destruct. Instead, the rejected one returns, forgives, and says he will be with us always! *This* prophet not only preached the message of our Father, but as the risen one he also manifests that he is with God in an intimate manner. Human Jesus is named the "son of God." Given Jesus' human-divine story—the Creed's "true God *and* true man"—humanity is inextricably linked in brotherhood and sisterhood to Jesus and his Father. That embarrassing relative we wanted to get rid of moves permanently into our history. Once and for all he blocks us from denying a family connection to our divine parent. Jesus returns as the forgiving one and affirms that, no matter how we may seek to forget and break the family bond, God remains with us, waiting eagerly for our return to the family home. Jesus is our family link to the forgiving Father who hastens to greet his returning prodigal.

Christian faith, then, is larger and deeper than morality; it is a vision of the world and history caught up in a cosmic family drama. In what sense is the Bible "history"? This is a complicated issue involving the very meaning of "history" as the defining character of being human. It is *being-historical* that differentiates humanity from the rest of creation. There is a "history" to the evolution of the horse, but horses are not historical actors. Without delving the depths of what it means to have a history at all, one can certainly see that the Bible fits the literary genre of history. Biblical criticism has insisted over the past several centuries, however, that it hardly presents history in terms of verified or verifiable fact. Much biblical "history" is downright false, and this understanding has led to the notion that it may all be fable. A spiritually enlightening fable, perhaps, but not essentially different than Dickens. Christian orthodoxy obviously does not accept the reduction of the Bible to elevating fiction. In some way, Creation and Resurrection are deeply true in "fact" though it may be quite obscure as to how to describe or account for such "facts." Conversations may be invented, emotions recounted, and facts alleged that did not actually occur because they capture the true meaning and spirit of an event which did occur. Whatever the *facts* of Resurrection, something happened to the disciples that was remembered in that fashion. The disciples did not make up a story from whole cloth to comfort their guilt or to teach a lesson. Something happened to them that was recounted as the event of Resurrection.

The Church is not, then, a school of biblical morals; it is an ongoing family saga. Though it may be God's family, it is carried forward by humans and is, like all human families, sometimes, often, frequently, always dysfunctional. Nevertheless, here we are, stuck in the family as it celebrates and quarrels through the ages. Any "moral" instruction that the Christian family (Church) may offer—abortion morality as just one instance—must be understood as a moment within the great world story of humanity. The "moral" question in the Bible is whether our individual story is worthy within God's family history. In ordinary life, we all understand how one can disappoint family history. How, then, are we to act in our ultimate family, God's family? How does God's history, as well as Jesus' life, death, and resurrection, speak to our own particular, idiosyncratic, often very quirky histories?

Telling Stories and "Objective" Morality

Shifting perspective to individual human stories within the spirit of the biblical story raises again the problem of "objective morality." As previously discussed, "objective" morality is often interpreted as judging actions in the manner of a scientist—a procedure that produces universal assent about the truth of the matter at hand. To accomplish this goal, the scientist abstracts himself or herself from all personal characteristics in order to obtain an "objective" viewpoint. Scientific laws are not colored by the ancestry of the scientist. Einstein was disdained by many German physicists because he practiced "Jewish physics." It is not only the scientific observer who is "abstract," but the subject observed is also abstract. Objective science is interested in the abstract type, not the individual. We have a biological science of the species *Homo sapiens*, because we are concerned with the type. As species types, Socrates, St. Theresa of Avila, and Genghis Kahn are all the same.

One could claim that the proper approach to ethics demands a similar objective stance. Actions are assessed from a universal standpoint beyond the moralist's personal and particular history. If the moralist is "above" his or her particular history, so also is the action assessed removed from any particular history. Morality is universal; it is not an expression of this or that person, this or that history, this or that culture—it is a view outside of time and place: a God's-eye view. From such a notion of objective morality, it is easy to claim that the Bible offers a universal moral law because it is, after all, morality from a God's-eye view. The Bible contains God's moral lessons with an historical wrapping. This view inverts the relation between morality and history in the Bible. The history is not a coating for a morality; the morality is what we gather from the history. For all that the Ten Commandments may be God's moral injunction, the Ten Commandments respond to the specific story of Creation and the Exodus. It is the history of Creation and Exodus that provides the "stance" of the Commandments. As the First Commandment says, "I am the Lord your God who brought you out of the house of Egypt, out of the land of slavery; you shall have no other Gods before me." It is God's intervention in Jewish history that leads to the Ten Commandments. The Ten Commandments are the work of *this* biblical God—they are not as such "objective" moral views that can be abstracted from their historic setting.

When people say that they accept the Ten Commandments as general moral prescriptions, they usually mean only the last six or seven (depending on whatever version of *the* Ten Commandments one's denomination favors). The God of the Exodus and the demands of the Sabbath are left out. The New Testament can be constricted to something like the Beatitudes. These readings replace the Creator and the God of the Exodus with a moral teacher; Jesus the savior with Jesus the moralist. In the Bible we are not facing a transcendent teacher of "objective morality." The Jewish and Christian God is too mixed up in time and history to play the role of the impersonal, transcendent, ahistorical moral tutor. What is "objective" in the Bible is the *definitive history of God-for-humanity*. "Moral" judgment is deciding how my particular history fits in God's history-for-humanity, whether my story can be read as humanity-for-God.

I repeat what was discussed in the chapter on morality: questioning the notion of "objective" morality in the Bible is not an open door to "subjective" morality of wish and whim. The issue for the Bible is "Who are you? What sort of person are you?" One must not confuse being a *subject*, a definite person, with *subjective*. As a *subject* my *person* is not "subjective" in the sense of something I alter as the moment, taste, or fashion might occasion. If I am "subjective" in that sense, then I would be a very definite sort of person: an untrustworthy and vacillating person.

God as Author

The Bible story starts with Creation, and Creation sets its basic theme. For that reason it is important to understand the special sense of biblical Creation and God as Creator. A common view of the Creator is that he is a sort of divine engineer who designed and brought forth the sun and the moon, the sea and the land, the plants and animals, and then, finally, human beings. These creations can be described in the clear naturalistic terms such as we find in physics or biology. Human beings, however, seem oddly placed in the natural world. Unlike the animals, we continually transcend (or violate) our biological nature. As noted above, we have not only a "natural history" like the evolution of the horse, but we also have a "cultural" history unique to our species. Humans invent medicine to thwart the natural process of disease; we create morality to check "animal" instincts. The human community seems better defined by its history, art, and culture than its biology, whether it is the art of agriculture or argumentation. The difference between humanity in nature and humanity in history is critical for moral discourse.

For biological nature, sexual parts have their fixed function. Human beings have, however, invented "the art of love," which embeds sexual function within interpersonal relation and meaning. It is because we go beyond nature in husbandry and husbanding that we think of ourselves as "persons," beings who are defined by special histories, particular choices, and unique accomplishments. Among the inhabitants of the local planet, only human beings are persons, only human beings live in history. It is the human fall or ascent into history that makes official Catholic "natural law" theory problematic. We assess humans from their history, not their biological structure.

Introducing history changes how we locate morality. It is simple enough to derive an objective and universal morality from biology, but the price one pays is assigning individual persons and their histories to their natural functions. If humanity is better understood through history and the arts, it is more illuminating to understand the Creator of the Bible not as a designer of nature (Designer-God), but as an author of a story (Author-God). God is not the "super-engineer" but rather the "super-playwright." The last thing that a playwright wants to create are characters who are mere types. In a moralistic play, we know from the minute the characters appear how they will act. A bad playwright fails to create *live* persons. A good playwright creates characters of such inner complexity and energy that they are living, real personalities for all that they play the villain or the hero. Macbeth is a villain, but with a terrifying vitality that no stock villain can command.

It is common for authors to say that the characters in their works "take on a life of their own." The distinguished Shakespearean critic Harold Bloom says that Hamlet and Falstaff exceed the limits of the play. In a sense, great fictional characters create their own personalities in a manner that finally eludes the author's original intent or control. The biblical doctrine of Creation conceives an Author-God, a God of story, a God of history, who creates real, live persons with proper names like Abraham and Sarah, Mary and Joseph. A Creator Author-God is the only God who makes sense of the fact that the Bible is a narrative. The Bible from Creation to Resurrection to Judgment is a relation of live persons to a personal God. The biblical God relates to every human being in the living reality of his or her unique history.

Abortion and Author-God

Assessing abortion biblically depends on what sort of God one has in mind. Biological design alone would make abortion a clear violation of natural process. An Author-God recasts the question from biological function into the life stories of individual persons. Shifting moral issues to the story of God's family and our individual stories within that history radically changes the abortion issue. Insisting on the abortion *story* is a check on both pro-life and pro-choice advocates since both can treat the issue at a high level of abstraction: abortion is abortion is abortion—and murder is all there is to it. Abortion is abortion is abortion—and choice is all there is to it. One denies the importance of a story; the other says that any old story will do. Recognizing the essential role of an abortion story does not justify any and all abortions—it changes the question from "Is it an abortion?" to "What is *this* abortion story?"

A woman makes her decision about pregnancy and possible abortion by assessing the local world as she finds it, and how her life situation relates to that world. We, in turn, judge her decision by how we understand the world and her situation. The possibilities for misreading the local world and her personal situation are manifest. Both can be misread: "Your situation is not *that* bad; you do have the personal strength to handle this crisis." Moral conversation is important for proper reading of world and self. The goal of ordinary moral deliberation is to find the best story for the woman considering her personal strengths and possibilities within the world as she finds it.

All well and good, but a pro-life critic will ask, "What about the story of the fetus?" Abortion doesn't just color that story—it finishes it off before it even starts. The question is appropriate insofar as it recognizes the moral claim of the fetus, but it fails to properly assess the moral situation presented in a pregnancy story. Strictly speaking, the woman is the only one who has a moral story. It is only in the woman's story that there are motives and circumstances that can enter into moral evaluation. Only the woman has a specific life story from which one might condemn or justify an abortion. If one extends a sense of mercy to the women in the concentration camp, it is because of *their* situation that judgment is colored and withheld. Unless one is prepared to regard abortion strictly as a physical act, a statutory offense, we are required in moral assessment to understand the story of the woman.

The World Story

The insistence on story repeats in a different mode the comments in the previous chapter about the importance of understanding *circumstance* in judging the morality of abortion. Biblical story expands "circumstance" beyond an immediate situation to the *life story* the woman is constructing in her decision. Assessing an abortion by introducing the circumstances of pregnancy embeds the woman in a complex of personal factors (age, health, psychological condition) and external situation (rape, incest). It sketches an immediate story but, from the biblical point of view, that story must finally be projected within the life story of the woman as she sees her story within the story of God, a "creation" story.

Everyday legal and moral judgment considers culpability in terms of the circumstances that create a story but these stories have a limited scope. One may in a particular case delve into the longer history of the individual to understand and excuse the action being judged. The individual is an abuser because he was abused. Whether the past history not only explains the deed but also excuses it is a matter of complex judgment. When one turns to action in the light of the Bible, the individual story is placed within the largest scope, into a world story, the story of God's family. The moral question: was my deed appropriate within the fundamental world story in which humans find themselves?

Take the case of the Jewish women who obtained abortions in the concentration camps. What sort of world were they in? Clearly their local world was as hostile as one could imagine. One could also believe that "hostile world" is not just a local story but the world story. When Elie Wiesel's fictional Holocaust survivor shuts his eyes, he feels he is in hostile territory. Perhaps it is not just the specific Nazi atrocity that shadows a limited class of survivors, but the Holocaust is also *the* story of human history, the ultimate story in which we all stand. The merest glance at history would suggest the scenario is frighteningly plausible. If Holocaust is the fundamental history within which we stand, how might that affect someone's attitude toward pregnancy? A strange question? Not at all. Elie Wiesel has written that he was very reluctant to father a child. Why bring new life into a world determined to slaughter the innocent? Wiesel's wife finally persuaded him to have hope for the future; he became a father. A darker story occurs in Federico Fellini's landmark film *La Dolce Vita*. A depressed intellectual, convinced that the world is on the brink of terror and destruction, kills his children and commits suicide.

Beyond the ups and downs of secular history, Judaism and Christianity preach an ultimate vision of the world in which we find ourselves. The Christian claim is that we exist in a world of Creation and Redemption. When I enact the Christian life and follow Christian "morality," it is because I believe that I am standing in a redeemed world. Christian history presents a paradoxical contrast to a Holocaust world. Despite the fact that Christianity's central symbol is the atrocity of the Cross, it proclaims that we live in a redeemed world of hope beyond despair for future children or suicide. The redemptive vision of hope is not a Christian idiosyncrasy; it is deep in the belief of Judaism despite that community's long history of exile, persecution, and pogrom. The Jewish worldview directly affects the issue of pregnancy. Franz Rosenzweig, the great modern Jewish theologian, said, "[The] belief [of the Jew] is not the content of a testimony, but rather the product of a reproduction. The Jew, engendered a Jew, attests his belief by continuing to procreate the Jewish people. His belief is not in something; he is himself the belief." A deep Jewish faith in the gracious Creator or Christian faith in the Resurrection of Jesus creates a self of everlasting hope. There is no *ultimate* justification for denying our life or new life because the world is hostile and utterly irredeemable. Both Orthodox Judaism and Catholicism are deeply procreational. Pregnancy stories are finally to be bound up in a world defined by hope.

But the local world as we find it *is* hostile. Even at best we are not living in communities and circumstances which realize the gracious openness of a redeemed world. More often than not we find ourselves in situations that do not even approximate the actions of a redeemed community. How should pregnancy and abortion be evaluated in the clash between the ultimate framework of biblical hope and actual Holocaust? How should a Jewish woman express Rosenzweig's procreational view of faith in a concentration camp?

One need not inflate particular situations to world-historical events like Nazi repression. There are household disasters where a woman is trapped in an inescapable cycle of abuse. How are we to understand hope in the great disasters of history and intimate tragedies of daily life? There are two sayings that can illuminate the issue of hope: "Where there's life there's hope" and "Where there's hope there's life." The first saying is commonplace. At the invalid's bedside we may think this a sensible attitude. When facing a tedious task, we may think that as long as we have the physical wherewithal, there's hope it will be completed. "Where there's hope there's life" speaks to the world of the spirit, not the body. To be without hope is to despair of life itself. The suicide acts out of despair. It may be despair over bodily decay, but more often it is really despair about the self. Even when physically healthy, no matter how successful we may be, we can be overcome by an inner sense of worthlessness, the futility of life. I suggest that the Jewish women in the concentration camp chose abortion out of hope. Utter despair would dictate death: "What does it matter if I die with my baby? All is lost, the world is eternally dark."

The Jewish and Christian vision of the world is a vision of ultimate hope: where there is hope there is life. Even at death, the believer lives in hope. Not hope for just more biological life—that is the wish on the sickbed—but for a fulfilled life to come that solves and salves the dilemmas of our earthly life.

Faith, Hope, and Love

"Where there is hope there is life" is, for Judaism and Christianity, more than a brave stance in the face of the eternal dark. Biblical hope is grounded in love and faith that penetrate the dark: "The light that shineth in the darkness." Despite the multiple and detailed moral instructions set down by the Church or derived from biblical passages, the underlying Christian demand is to exercise the virtues of faith, hope, and love. Conduct that contradicts these virtues is basic sin, Christian "moral" failure. It is important to understand all three terms as special biblical virtues; they are not to be amalgamated to the general character traits with the same names. What distinguishes the *biblical* virtues is their interconnection. The special character of biblical morality can be sensed from Jesus' answer to the lawyer who asks him, "Teacher, which commandment in the law is the greatest?" Jesus quotes traditional rabbinic teaching: "'You shall love the Lord your God with all your heart, and with all your soul, and all your mind.' This is the greatest and first commandment. And the second is like it: 'You shall love your neighbor as yourself'" (Matthew 22:36–38). If the average goodhearted person were to assess the two commandments, he or she would likely start with "love your neighbor," but have doubts about the need for loving God with your whole heart and soul. Indeed, a person may be concerned that loving God so extravagantly will leave little for the neighbor. Faith in God is not readily seen as necessary for the good life. The Bible, on the other hand—as Jesus' answer above indicates—grounds everything in God. What is the logic of this inversion of common opinion?

I have insisted in this presentation that Christian morality is not a standalone set of discrete moral commands derived from Scripture or our rational nature. Biblical morality is a function of "the world as we find it." For Christians the world as we find it is the world of the Creator, Jesus' Father and our Father. It is because of faith, belief that the world is the Creator's world, that hope and love make sense. Love and hope are ultimately grounded in the "fact" that the world is redeemed. We do not live finally on "a darkling plain . . . where ignorant armies clash by night." Belief in a Creator may be difficult, but it is more difficult to believe that a Creator of the world as we find it is to be loved with all one's heart, mind, and soul. The world as we find it more often seems to be that darkling plain. In a world of unrelieved conflict and hostility, hope and love can seem radically out of place. Look after yourself; the neighbor can do the same. Don't hope for too much and you won't be disappointed. Make the world as we find it "darkling" enough and bringing forth children seems pointless, and suicide is to be commended. Have no faith in the world as we find it and despair is almost a moral demand. I would not insist that biblical faith is necessary for hope and love. Albert Camus was a nonbeliever who saw hope and love as courageous defiance of the indifference and hostility of the world as we find it. Tellingly, Camus said the moral question every day was "Why should I not commit suicide?" Perhaps there are only three ultimate attitudes to the world as we find it: despair, defiance, or devotion—faith in the world as ultimately redeemed and redeemable.

Culture of Life

In the Book of Deuteronomy, God lays out a basic choice for humanity: "I have set before you life and death, blessing and curse; therefore choose life that you and your descendants may live" (Deuteronomy 30:19). What is Yahweh up to? Of course the Israelites need to be alive now so that they can have descendants later on. The dead do not propagate. Assuming that God is not given to making trite comments, he must have something more in mind than pointing out the facts of biological life. Choosing life is more than choosing healthy function. If God is an Author-God, he wants people who choose to live, not just to exist. Like the good playwright, he wants live characters not stock types to act on the great world stage. The Author-God wants people of passion and compassion, struggling to create lives that are open, creative, fruitful, loving—and this all too often means lives that are threatening and threatened, dangerous and endangered. The biblical God's "culture of life" asks for more than biological existence.

Framing the pro-life/pro-choice quarrel in the terms set forth in Deuteronomy one should ask to what extent the two views reflect a choice for life. Pro-life is fixated on biological life. Is the commitment to bringing forth biological life the same as committing to life? It certainly can be and one supposes most often it is. I have never seen my wife more radiant than when she held our newborn daughters in her arms. Parenting is a demanding and difficult challenge to life as easy drift; being a good parent is living *life*. Even if a pregnancy is unplanned, even forced upon a woman by custom or worse, a woman may rise to the challenge of investing her pregnancy with life, facing birth and beyond with courage and deep compassion. Because pregnancy is such a critical moment in the life of a woman, it offers a woman multiple rich ways to live life.

Can the choice for an abortion—a choice against biological life—be a choice for life? It does not take much imaginative ingenuity to construct scenarios that would illustrate how carrying forward a pregnancy can destroy a woman's life. Pregnancy imposed by rape, a partner's threatening demand, cultural pressure, or even a serious lapse in judgment may impose a future on a woman that seriously diminishes her life. One of the great strengths of the pro-choice cause is the emphasis on the woman living her own life, making her own choices. Pregnancy must be a woman's choice if it is to be an expression of life. Pregnancy and motherhood as a state into which the woman drifts because everyone is doing it, because it is an imposed duty, because she can't think of any other course for her life, is not a move in the culture of life. Drift is a function of despair, a loss of life. A woman who saw her life justified only by pregnancy "dies" at menopause; her life is over.

Nuns who take a vow of chastity choose life by a different road than bringing forth life. In the Middle Ages, when women were often relegated by society to being pawns for cementing family alliances through marriage, the nunnery was many times the realm of freedom for women, the choice for life. I would not want to equate the choice of women religious with the choice of abortion, but both can remove a woman from impossible oppression. The abortion decision that seeks life by directly turning against life in the womb carries great spiritual risk, but in both cases it may be that the woman is reaching as best she can for life. One can also write drifting and despairing scenarios for abortion. The woman has a thoughtless sexual encounter and then simply accepts a permissive culture of abortion as a cure. Thoughtlessness leads to more thoughtlessness and a choice for life is bypassed.

I am inclined to say that the Author-God of the Bible story is "pro-choice." The problem with enlisting God in the culture war is that neither pro-life nor pro-choice reach *God's* "pro-choice." What God wants is *deep* choice, a life choice. Pro-choice seems unable or unwilling to distinguish genuine deep choices in which the whole course of a woman's life is bound up, and trivial or even downright immoral choice. Pro-life fails to accept the notion that abortion may reflect a deep life choice. Even if one accepts the notion that the fetus has significant moral status, a woman may have to make a tragic choice against this potential life. Tragic choice is tragic because it is a deep life choice. The woman summons the full range of her powers, arrays them against the disastrous situation that threatens to destroy not her biological life, but her value and person. Choosing her person, she chooses life.

Chapter Six

Notable Lacks and Present Temptations

If I have had the good fortune by now to persuade the reader that an absolute condemnation of abortion is futile in law and inadequate in morals, the question that lingers is why Catholics have committed themselves to such an absolutist crusade. If, as this book claims, the Church's teaching is misleading at best, and downright mistaken at worst, one can ask why the Church's official teachers, popes, bishops, clerics, and conservative commentators get it wrong. American bishops have certainly not been shy in leading Catholic opinion on abortion nor in public censure of Catholics—particularly politicians—who, in the judgment of the censuring cleric, deviate from Church norms. I believe that their anti-abortion campaign is mistaken in its pursuit of legal prohibition and excessive in its moral condemnation. Why are the bishops acting so "irrationally"? If their reasons don't work, are there external factors that skew judgment? Are there factors within the current life and practice of Church leadership that distort judgment? I asked one of the most distinguished Church historians what was causing all this overheated episcopal rhetoric. Without hesitation, he said, "Anger." "What are they angry about?" I asked, genuinely puzzled. "Everything," he replied.

One can easily construct a list of things that vex the bishops. The scandal of pedophile priests, while it has led to some moving moments of penitence, has also provoked episcopal outrage at the media, which, they claim, sensationalized the issue. Incessant press coverage, often of cases long past, has cast a pall over the priesthood and unfairly implicated the innocent. There are many signs of Catholic Church diminishment: the drastic decline in vocations to the priesthood and religious life, dwindling congregations, the closing of churches, and rejection by the faithful of what the authorities consider central truths, such as the ban on artificial birth control. While more Americans indicate "Catholic" as their faith than any other religion, the second-largest number identify themselves as "former Catholics." It is a common enough reaction for those who lose position and prestige to lash out in anger. The bishops and the Church have suffered such a loss in the past decades.

Whatever the reason, anger is certainly part of the anti-abortion rhetoric. There is a bitterness toward and disdain of opposing points of view—often most vehemently directed at other Catholics who beg to disagree. Moral discourse is not improved by anger, and its display in a religious community urged to "love your enemies" seems particularly out of place. Sometimes I think that the bishops "love" enemies because they present an opportune target on which to vent their fears and frustration.

Anger often searches for a scapegoat, an enemy within or without that can be blamed for the fall from grace. The enemy has been spotted: "It is not Catholic faith that is at fault; it is the pernicious influence of liberalism, secularism, and moral relativism." In the words of the conservative Catholic commentator George Weigel, what is needed is "the courage to be Catholic," rejection of the false philosophies of modernism, and a return to obedience to the pope and the *magisterium* in Rome. Weigel even accounts for priest pedophilia by faulting the failure of the American bishops to discipline the priests who publicly protested *Humanae Vitae*. By allowing these priests with "liberal" sexual agendas to continue to serve, sexual restraint overall loosened and pedophilia was the result. Abortion is the final sum and manifestation of sexual license and pernicious modernity, the coming of "the culture of death."

Whatever displaced anger may contribute to the tone of the anti-abortion campaign, there are certain aspects of Catholic practice, structure, and culture that contribute to the character of the Church's current position on abortion. None of these factors alone is the direct cause for the Church's opposition, but I believe that they provide a background that colors the arguments and heats the rhetoric. There is no necessary connection between male celibacy of Catholic clergy and the Church's insensitivity to a woman's issue like abortion, but one suspects that it is no help.

This chapter will concentrate on aspects of Church leadership, from parish priest to pope, that contribute to the high rhetoric of anti-abortion, but it is also necessary to say a word about lay Catholics, many of whom are as ardent in opposition to abortion as the most outspoken cleric. If Catholic leadership seems quick to locate enemies abroad, many Catholic faithful may be quick to agree. The American Catholic experience has been an immigrant experience, immigration into a determinedly Protestant world that deeply distrusted Catholics and, quite often, the nationality of the believers. The result was the creation of "ghetto Catholicism" with its parallel universe of schools, hospitals, and social services. Catholics clung to their Church with a special fervor not only because it was "the true Church" but because it spoke to their national experience—often in the native tongue. We are long past the days when signs read "Irish need not apply," but a sense of specialness of *Catholic* commitment lingers on. What is surprising is not so much that the second-largest religious group is "former Catholics," but the fact that Catholics continue as Catholics despite all sorts of disagreements with the leadership and dissents from Vatican dicta. Why don't Catholics who use contraception or long for women priests just up and join the Episcopalians? The peculiar stick-to-it attitude of Catholics offers fertile ground for the sort of "locate the enemy" preaching of Church authorities. Catholics may not have "the courage to be Catholic" full and entire in the mode of George Weigel, but they hang in there. Catholics may not agree with the strictures of the bishops—a majority of Catholics did, after all, vote for "pro-choice" Obama—but they seldom offer public dissent. The demographics of the American Catholic population are shifting, but the new Catholics—many Latinos, some Asians—are generally "conservative," and unlikely to lead dissent to official teaching. There is much talk by bishops and priests about the importance of the laity to the future of the American Church. This talk is supported by the reality of a priest shortage and the assumption of many pastoral duties by lay ministries. What is lacking, however, is any clear, public, "official" structure or practice for incorporating broader lay participation in the decisions of the hierarchy. Thus, for the time being, official opinion as stated by popes, bishops, and the local priest appears to be *the* Catholic opinion, however much the parishioner in the pew disagrees.

Lacks and Temptations

Episcopal opinion without notable dissent from below dominates the abortion debate. I want to examine some of the external factors that can affect the attitudes and beliefs of clerical leadership. I make no claim that the factors chosen are either individually or collectively solely responsible for the Church's position on abortion. I can only say that they appear to be worthy of comment. They are impediments that must be overcome, dangers to be avoided, if the Church is to assess the abortion issue in its full reality. I have grouped the problems into two large headings: "Lacks" and "Temptations"—three "lacks" (lack of experience, lack of listening, and lack of education), and three "temptations" (the temptation of morality, the temptation of science, and the temptation of religion). These six factors often interact with one another to create a concerted view of the Church. If you are a conservative like George Weigel, you will regard these factors not as lacks or temptations but as essential to the very meaning of Church. Celibacy for the priesthood is not an impediment, it is the proper expression of the Eucharistic presider in the *imago Christi*, and so on. For conservatives, the factors link together into a coherent Christian system. My own view is that they merge into a psychological syndrome that leads to aberrant ecclesiastical behavior. As system or syndrome these factors particularly affect the hierarchy.

Should a secular reader of this book or a non-Catholic be interested in the facts or foibles of the "Roman system"? I think so. One could cite the New Testament injunction: "Why do you see the speck in your neighbor's eye, but do not notice the beam in your own eye?" (Matthew 7:3). I leave it to the reader to decide which side, pro-life or pro-choice, has the speck and which the beam, but both sides would do well to consider external factors that drive the debate to excess. Insofar as these lacks and temptations color the abortion argument, recognition of the problems they pose for communication might actually improve dialogue. If I have a sense of where my interlocutor is "coming from"—as the phrase goes—I am better able to shape a constructive conversation. Because this person lives a certain sort of life, there will be ranges of experience that will resonate in conversation and others that will fall flat. If I am talking to a married woman with a large family, I can easily appeal to life experiences that are just not there for a celibate male priest. He may, one hopes, be a person of expansive imagination, but that is to be discovered, not counted on. Since the Catholic Church is a formidable presence in the public square, it is useful to see what shapes its voice for good and for ill.

Before suggesting how the various lacks and temptations distort the Church's anti-abortion rhetoric and action, I want to reiterate what is clearly correct in the Church's position. If one is puzzled about why Catholics are pursuing an all-out anti-abortion campaign, the most generous reply is that there is a serious moral issue to be addressed. There are deep faults in a pervasive American culture of "do your own thing." Abortion as mere "choice" is a case in point. Church leadership is correct to insist that abortion poses grave moral issues. They are even correct to regard abortion as an "intrinsic evil." The fatal mistake has been failure to relate the moral problem of abortion to legal action, specifically criminalization. Plainly put, it seems clear that there is no acceptable way to create criminal law that measures up to the rhetoric of homicide and murder. In the South Dakota situation, the dioceses, however unconsciously, supported a criminal statute that clearly downgraded the moral rhetoric about abortion. Failure in criminal law suggests that, while abortion is an intrinsic evil, it lacks the moral weight suggested by the rhetoric of murder. Lacking that level of gravity, the abortion decision must be weighed against other moral considerations when adjudicating right and wrong.

Three Notable Lacks

Lack of Experience: Outsiders and Insiders

One of the factors that pushes Church leaders (specifically, the hierarchy) toward absolutism on the abortion issue is a lack of pastoral experience. Jesus commanded Peter, "Feed my sheep!" Popes and bishops have taken on the mantle of *pastors* to the Catholic flock. Given that role, one can ask just what sort of "pastoral" experience they bring to the post. In the New Testament, the good shepherd is the one who searches for the one lost sheep. That may be what happens at the parish level, but is that possible at the diocesan chancery office or in a Vatican dicastery? (The arcane names themselves suggest some distance from the individual sheep out there.) How much pastoral experience, one on one with the ordinary faithful, has Church leadership enjoyed? How about the supreme pastor, the bishop of Rome—the pope?

Popes

There have been popes and there have been popes; one can hardly sum up two thousand years of papal pastoral experience. If I consider the popes of my own lifetime they present a mixed picture. The dominant pope of my early years was Eugenio Pacelli, Pius XII, who reigned from 1939 to 1958. Pius's experience prior to his elevation to the papacy was exclusively in the Vatican diplomatic core, rising to be cardinal secretary of state. Giovanni Montini, who reigned as Paul VI from 1963 to 1978, served in the Vatican diplomatic corps from 1922 to 1954, when he was appointed to be archbishop of Italy's largest diocese, Milan.

There is much to be admired in the activities of these two papacies. Pius XII liberated Catholic biblical studies; Paul VI successfully concluded Vatican II. There is also much to question: Pius XII's dubious record during the Holocaust; Paul VI's vacillation in the implementation of Vatican II. Popes bring certain virtues to their office, but often the vices of their virtues as well. Given the world scope of the Roman Catholic Church and its complex structure, long experience in Vatican diplomacy, such as that enjoyed by Pius XII and Paul VI, was obviously a strength. On the other hand, it may also account for the problems of their papacies. Astute commentators on Pius XII have suggested that part of his failure to deal adequately with the Holocaust was a result of his diplomatic turn of mind. Nazi genocide was not an evil to be dealt with diplomatically—it demanded denunciation. Paul VI faced serious tensions between traditionalists and progressives after Vatican II. He attempted to solve the conflict diplomatically by appointing traditionalists and progressives into the same offices at the Vatican, expecting them to negotiate agreement. They did not. Depending on whether one supports conservatives or progressives, one would have preferred decisive direction instead of the indecision that led Paul to be characterized as the "Hamlet of the Vatican."

A long diplomatic career does not in itself lead to vacillation or negotiating the nonnegotiable. John XXIII (Angelo Roncalli), who succeeded Pius XII, was a very different person and pope from his autocratic predecessor or his shy successor, Paul VI. Personal history may, of course, explain some of one's behavior as pope: John was the son of peasants, while Pius came from an aristocratic family with long ties to the Vatican. Like Pius and Paul, John XXIII had a long diplomatic career, but his assignments in such out of the way places (to the Vatican) as Bulgaria and Turkey isolated him from the infighting of the Roman curia. When he was nuncio in France, he made it a practice to have dinner once a week with an ordinary family. Roncalli's non-establishment ancestry, offbeat diplomatic postings, and personal warmth probably helped foster the spirit of openness to the world that marked the second Vatican Council, which he convened. Despite minimal parish experience, John XXIII displayed a pastoral outreach that led to his being dubbed "the beloved John XXIII."

Karol Wojtyla, John Paul II, had immense pastoral gifts that were clearly on display in many of his worldwide tours and his opening to the Jewish community. Some of that pastoral energy was derived from experience of the Church-besieged in his native Poland. In Communist Poland one could hardly be a bureaucrat content to negotiate with those determined to destroy the Church. Unfortunately, he brought his vision of a Church-in-opposition to the papal office, establishing a combative stance that quite reversed the openness to the world that John XXIII brought from his experience.

The current pope elected in 2005, Benedict XVI (Joseph Ratzinger), has a different background than any of his immediate predecessors. After a notable and prolific twenty-five-year academic career in dogmatic theology, he served five years as archbishop of Munich-Freising before coming to Rome in 1981 to head the Congregation for the Doctrine of the Faith (CDF). His speeches and writings as pope clearly demonstrate a theological depth and clarity of expression that is admirable. His problems in communication have occurred when he fails to distinguish the sort of in-house academic setting of his professorial life and the broader audience that will react to his remarks.

In one way or another, these popes were either "insiders" who knew the ropes of the papal bureaucracy, as did Pius XII and Paul VI, or outsiders like John XXIII and John Paul II whose formative experience lay beyond Roman politics. Benedict XVI is a double insider: a theologian skilled in the arcane talk of academics and a long-time head of a Vatican office. It was appropriate for John XXIII to quip when asked "How many people work in the Vatican?," "About half." That seems to be how he treated the bureaucracy. They were only to be taken half-seriously when he wanted to reach out to the modern world in an ecumenical council. John Paul II seems to have ignored the insiders in a different way. He has been criticized for spending time outside Rome evangelizing rather than running the central office. Left to itself by a touring pope, the Roman curia, like all bureaucracies, guarded the status quo, to the detriment of the reformist impulses of Vatican II.

There is no easy solution to the need in the complicated, worldwide, hierarchical Church of combining "managerial" skill with the pastoral touch, an insider/outsider dilemma. Only one pope has ever resigned: Celestine V. In 1294 the papacy had been vacant for over two years while the cardinals quarreled over a successor. They were admonished by a holy hermit, Pietro di Morone, to settle the matter. The cardinals responded by electing Pietro as pope. He arrived from his hermitage riding a donkey. The ultimate outsider, utterly baffled by the intrigues of the papal court, he resigned five months later and returned to his cell. Celestine was succeeded by one of the great wheeler-dealer insider popes, Boniface VIII. As Benedetto Catetani he had served the previous thirty years in the Roman curia. For good reasons no subsequent pope has taken the name of Celestine.

Bishops

If one turns to the experience of current diocesan bishops, few of them have come from a holy hermit's cell or even extensive parish work. The Catholic Church has what the Latins called a *cursus honorum,* the road to honor (promotion); it lies through an early accession to the bureaucracy from the local diocese on up to Rome. This makes sense but raises the significant problem for all organizations of separating management from the workers (parish priests) and customers (the laity). One bishop who was conscious of the dilemma of manager-and-pastor was the late Kenneth Untener of the diocese of Saginaw, Michigan. When he became bishop, Untener sold the episcopal residence—often referred to as the episcopal "palace" in other dioceses. He then commuted from one parish to the next, living there for a week or so, getting to know his priests and people. He carried his bureaucratic work with him in his car. Untener was one of the "Jadot bishops" and as such was a favorite target of conservative Catholics who believe that the Jadot bishops destroyed true Catholicism in the United States.

Lack of grassroots experience may account for a significant disconnect between the episcopal hierarchy and significant portions of the laity. Why, after all, do most Catholics reject the teaching on birth control? It does not fit to their actual experience, whatever the official Church may say about its intrinsic evil. There is also a disconnect between parish priests and many of their bishops. In olden days, bishops were often elected by priests from the local diocese. The priests knew their bishop and he knew them. Today, bishops are appointed largely on the recommendation of other bishops, a sign-off from the papal nuncio, and Vatican action. The recent pedophilia scandals have deepened the gulf between priests and bishops. Priests believe they have been the "fall guys" while bishops who covered up abuse have, by and large, gone scot-free.

Women

Lack of pastoral experience is a problem for the hierarchy, but there is the general problem for all Catholic clergy: lack of experience with women—an issue of special sensitivity for the issue of abortion. However much a bishop may or may not have had pastoral experience, the fact is that his official life is lived in an enclave of an all-male, celibate organization. Whatever learning by experience males may acquire through marriage and sexuality is precluded. Even if, after long marriage and an active sexual life, a male concludes, as he often does, that women are something of a mystery, that would be a salutary check on making definitive rules and pronouncements governing the female sex. Christian understanding is directed to the mystery of the individual soul, so knowing individual souls, the lone sheep, is essential. The Church is structured to exclude the immediate experiences of women, most obviously in the review, formulation, and proclamation of policy. Women are just not present at the decision-making level of the Church. Whatever insights and experience they might bring to bear are lacking or, as the next section suggests, ignored when offered.

The historical record shows that Catholicism has had a continuing problem in understanding the moral and spiritual needs of women. There have been repeated problems over the centuries, from the medieval Beguines to the nineteenth-century Sisters of Mercy, when communities of women have attempted to establish their own manner of action or worship. The story continues: at the time of the writing of this book, the Vatican has announced not one but two separate investigations of the conduct and orthodoxy of American women religious. There was no prior consultation with these religious communities; the "visitation" was imposed for reasons that remain obscure. When, in the recent past, women religious have expressed their sense of calling to priestly ministry, they were instructed by John Paul II that the topic was not even to be discussed.

The Church hierarchy suffers, then, from a double burden in understanding the reality of the abortion issue. Those who manage the Church and make the rules come to positions of authority without much direct experience with the actual life of the faithful. Second, the clergy is made up of celibate males who have little contact with women in the range and depth of their capabilities and experiences.

Lack of Listening: "He That Hath Ears, Let Him Hear" (Mark 4:9)

Experience isn't everything. No male can have the experience of a pregnant woman or the travails of abortion. There are lots of human experiences we not only cannot have, but do not want to have for any reason whatsoever: the pain of cancer or the immorality of bitter hatred. Nevertheless, it can be very important that we learn what we can about behavior beyond our own possibilities or desires. Doctors want to understand as best they can the pain of their patients; criminologists are interested in the experience of felons. One way that we learn about the experience of others is by listening to stories about experiences we do not share. If the Catholic hierarchy cannot have the experience of women and would not, if they could, countenance the experience of an abortion, they could at least listen to women on that score. I recount one such attempt and its consequences from the autobiography of Rembert Weakland O.S.B., who was at the time archbishop of Milwaukee. The quotation sums up much of the problem of the bishops and abortion. He recounts attending a meeting of the National Council of Catholic Bishops (NCCB), predecessor to the USCCB.

> At their fall 1989 meeting, the bishops of the United States passed a resolution condemning abortion, a statement I supported. After the meeting, as I nestled down in my seat . . . for the flight from Washington to Milwaukee, something about the meeting began to disturb me. Lingering in my mind was the image of the bishops, 280 gray-haired men, passing a resolution that they expected all American Catholics to embrace. My uneasiness grew: other than the conference staff, no lay people, especially no women, were part of the discussion vital to all, but especially to women in the Church. It occurred to me that, from a pastoral point of view, it would be helpful to listen to the women of my own archdiocese as they expressed their feelings on this difficult subject. A passage from Pope Paul VI's first encyclical, *Ecclesiam suam*, came to mind: "Before speaking we must take care to listen not only to what people say, but what they have it in their hearts to say."

Following through on this inspiration, Weakland organized six sessions with women to discuss a range of issues, including abortion. Representations were made in writing and in person by women who had had abortions. Weakland reports, "At no time did any woman say that abortion was a moral good; they all found it a moral evil. But their fears about a future in which it would become a criminal act was evident."

What was the result of the archbishop's initiative to listen? With the assistance of theologian Mary Feeley, the sessions' coordinator, Weakland wrote an essay that was published in the diocesan paper. Whatever good may have come from the sessions and the essay, no good came to the archbishop. In the summer of 1990, he was invited to receive an honorary degree by the theological faculty at the University of Fribourg in Switzerland. Part of the protocol in offering the degree was approval by Rome. The prefect in charge of this task, Archbishop Pio Laghi, formerly papal nuncio in the United States, denied permission. He stated that the hearings on abortion were "not without doctrinal importance" and had caused "a great deal of confusion among the faithful." So much for listening to women about abortion.

The Milwaukee conferences were by no means an isolated case of official lack of listening. In the 1980s, the U.S. Catholic bishops attempted to write a pastoral letter on women. To initiate the pastoral, listening sessions were held in the various dioceses. The experience of married women, the divorced, those who had had abortions, fervent Catholics, and those who were estranged were gathered. In the first draft of the pastoral, these varied voices were recorded. That was too much for Rome, which insisted on a more doctrinal presentation. A second draft appeared, without specific voices. Even that was too edgy and a third draft was ordered. Finally, it was decided that no pastoral should be issued. The effort was abandoned. The history of the failed pastoral may be emblematic. It seems that the Church has nothing to say to women—certainly not if it has to listen to the voice of their experience.

In advocating, as Paul VI did in *Ecclesiam suam*, that the bishops listen to those directly affected by their rulings, I am not thereby advocating a "democratic" Church. *Vox populi* is not *vox Dei*. But if the Church is in some sense a "teaching Church," it must also be a "learning Church," and one of the sources of learning is what the faithful "say in their hearts." Only if the Church speaks to the heart can it be heard. Cardinal Newman's episcopal motto captures the spirit of Christian teaching and learning: *cor ad cor loquitor* (heart speaks to heart).

The position of this book is very much what the women at Weakland's conferences expressed: "At no time did any woman say that abortion was a moral good; they all found it a moral evil. But their fears about a future in which it would become a criminal act was evident." Even at this date, those words from the heart are worth listening to.

Lack of Learning: Canon Law and Words From the Heart

Listening to the faithful—and the unfaithful—should be a vital moment of learning for the Church and its leadership, but it is not the only way of learning. Books are useful! The Catholic Church is blessed with what may be the most enriched body of learning of any religious communion: the writings of the Fathers, a variety of subtle philosophical and theological writings, mystical poetry, the history of saints, sophisticated biblical studies—even papal encyclicals. This intellectual tradition continues with vigor to the present day. It is remarkable how little of this literature is availed of by Church leadership. The formal training of priests consists in seminary theology—of which I will have more to say in due course—and, in the case of many bishops, canon law, or Church rules. Whether specially trained in canon law or not, as bishops, following the canons becomes a central task.

In a sample of current or recent cardinals, Cardinals Rigali, Bevilacqua, Keeler, Hickey, and Law all received advanced degrees in canon law from one of the Vatican universities. Cardinal Maida received a degree in civil law after joining the priesthood. Cardinal Law held degrees in canon and civil law. It makes sense that individuals charged with organizing and managing Church affairs should be trained in the laws of the Church, but what view of the Church does one obtain through the lens of canon law?

When Cardinal Joseph Bernardin of Chicago announced the formation of the Common Ground initiative to open dialogue between differing voices in the Church—"liberal" and "conservative," as these terms are often used—the project was immediately denounced by four of the other American cardinals. Public criticism by one cardinal of another is extraordinary. The critics stated that there was no need for conversation; difference suggested that one could in any way dissent from official teaching. The four who objected to Common Ground conversation were Cardinals Law, Hickey, Bevilacqua, and Maida—as noted, the first three were trained in canon law, and the last in civil law. Bernardin, who earlier wanted to be a physician, was not a canon lawyer; he had a graduate degree in theology. Cardinal Roger Mahony, who joined the Common Ground project, held a master's degree in social work. It is not a great stretch to suggest that the assumption of closure in canon law precluded the openness of conversation that Bernardin hoped to foster.

Canon law is not like the Constitution of the United States. The body of canon law is more a gathering than a single-minded construction. It was not until the eleventh century that any systematic collection was made of the various and varied rulings of ecumenical councils, local councils, biblical injunctions, "natural law" directives, papal statements, and so on. Subsequent popes over the centuries revised and reordered the canons. By the nineteenth century there were ten thousand norms, not all of which were consistent with one another. Pius X sought to have a single volume of stated law, but this task was not completed until 1917. Vatican II led to a further revision of canon law, which was issued in 1983. The current text contains 1,752 canons. The canons cover everything from "housekeeping" regulations (an advisory under Canon 13 on whether Catholics on cruise ships are obligated to attend Mass) to important moral concerns, such as Canon 1324 on the diminishment of penalty because of grave fear cited in the case discussed in chapter 4 about the abortion performed on the nine-year-old Brazilian girl.

Reading the Church through the lens of canon law presents an insider's view of the Church-as-organization. An insider view has its own limitations as suggested, and canon law may pose a further burden. At its worst, canon law has been a hodge-podge of inconsistent instruction. There is also the very effect of compilation: bringing disparate elements into a single, rationalized text suggests that all the canons are equally important for Christian life. After being cleaned up, canon law seems to collect rulings from the trivial to the sublime. Attending mass on a cruise ship cannot really be as important as weighing "grave fear" in making a moral assessment. Finally, the form of *law* can subtly distort Christian vision. Put simply—repeating my constant theme—Christian vision goes *to the person,* the heart, the unique *thou.* In the final analysis, which is, after all, God's analysis, human beings cannot be encased in law-like categories. A rose may be a rose, but humans resist such finality.

A bishop of my acquaintance, though trained in canon law, cautioned the priests in his diocese that in dealing with controversies like same-sex marriage and abortion, they should always remember that these are not just abstract issues—they are embedded in the lives and beliefs of individuals. He got that right. The USCCB got it right when it titled its pastoral on homosexuality "Always Our Children." When I chided the bishop about his background in canon law, expressing my concern that law gives only a limited vision of Christianity, he smiled and assured me that he also had a licentiate in sacred theology. Maybe that is what led him to caution his priests about the essential difference between abstract issues and the persons who live out those convictions, but I am inclined to think it rests more on his personality and pastoral sense.

Does theological training qualify the limitations of the law's vision? No priest in the Church can escape theological study and many of the hierarchy hold advanced theology degrees. Cardinal Egan of New York, despite his reputation for managerial aloofness, held a doctorate in canon law, but was also a licentiate in sacred theology. The question to be raised about clerical training in theology is about the *spirit* of that theology. Just what sort of intellectual endeavor is the theology offered in the seminary or advanced study—particularly in the special theological faculties licensed by the Vatican? Is such theological study open or closed, speculative or dogmatic, exploratory or defensive? Since my professional field is philosophy, which is at least a close relative of theology, I would be suspicious of anything called "licensed philosophy." If one looks at the great theological tradition of the Church, the aims of theology can seem far from anything that can be closed with certainty. The great Dominican theologian of the Middle Ages, Meister Eckhart, titled his work *The Cloud of Unknowing*. That doesn't sound like it would yield many hard dogmatic conclusions. When challenged to defend his orthodoxy, Eckhart claimed with some justification to be a disciple of St. Thomas Aquinas, who, at least since the declarations of Pope Leo XIII in the nineteenth century, has been designated the official philosopher-theologian of the Church.

If training in canon law can distort ecclesiastical vision away from the radical individuality of the I-Thou relation, theology in the wrong spirit can also descend into law-like conclusions and closed categories. Theology becomes a sort of supernatural knowledge yielding demonstration of such important matters as the existence of God and moral law. But is theology a way of knowing or, as Eckhart and a number of "mystical" theologians have suggested, a way of "unknowing"? Does theology expand our knowledge or humble the intellect before the God who says, "my thoughts are not your thoughts, neither are my ways your ways" (Isaiah 55:8)? It makes a great difference in the surety one may bring to Church statements—including moral teaching.

The spirit of theology is a subject that has to await full discussion when I move on to the temptation of science and religion in the next sections. For now, let me simply raise the suspicion that the theology in which priests and bishops receive formal training tends to be defensive theology—theology that creates a clarity to faith complementary to canon law. Clarity and law have their place for conserving the traditions and structures of the Church, but they lack openness to the always elusive ways of humankind.

Three Notable Temptations

Temptation of Morality: Morality and Miracles

It has been tempting to latch onto anti-abortion as an out-front Church position precisely *because* it is a serious moral issue. In the light of the widespread rejection by the faithful of the ban on artificial contraception, opposing abortion seems morally compelling. Furthermore, the Church can be tempted to preach general morality to avoid dealing with the more difficult biblical story.

There are obvious problems with preaching the biblical story in the modern secular age. Most people are deeply concerned about moral issues of some sort, but they are less and less inclined to accept stories about the Creation, Incarnation, and Resurrection. Faith claims seem quite contrary to common experience. While fundamentalists cite the Bible to justify morality, the liberal tendency in and out of the Church is to cite morality as the essential point of Scripture. Most people accept some variant of the Ten Commandments. Beyond the law there is significant approval of Jesus' sense of compassion, interest in the poor, and his message of love. One can have religion-as-morality and jettison the miracles.

The temptation to preach religion as morality is not a fault specific to Catholicism. Ever since modern biblical criticism questioned the historical veracity of biblical tales, various Christian denominations with various levels of acquiescence have opted for a moral reading of Scripture. Nineteenth-century "liberal Protestantism" is one relatively clear example. Confusing religion and morality is, however, as inappropriate as confusing art and morality or science and morality. Art, science, religion, and morality rest on differing basic assumptions that cannot be fused. It may be immoral to pursue stem-cell research, but it may be very good science. Religion's view of human destiny will certainly influence morality, but Christian morality depends on a "stance" about God and human history that is special to faith. Common morality plain or philosophic does not derive morality from a theology of history.

The very fact that abortion is *not* universally regarded as deeply immoral may make the position especially attractive to the Church. The prophets of Israel and Jesus preached against the morality of the day. Pro-life can wrap itself in prophetic robes as it stands for morality against selfishness and secularism. Prophets are not, however, moral reasoners. They *declare* the truth and brook no argument or qualification. Their claims are absolute. Christianity inherits prophetic religion and its absoluteness, but it is an absoluteness about God and history, not about morality as such. Catholicism is particularly identified with definitive "dogmatic" pronouncements on up to infallible truths promulgated by the pope. Dogma is essential to Christianity, but it needs to be understood as *religious* dogma. What, then, is the Church doing when it asserts *religious* dogma, or states *religious* truth? To answer that question, I need to take a brief detour to consider Pilate's question: "What is truth?"

The Temptation of Science: The Ghost of Descartes

"What is truth?" For many centuries the Bible was *the* standard of truth; it presented accurate history and cosmology. Long before critical historians undermined Scripture's historical accuracy, biblical cosmology had been rejected by modern natural science. Joshua did *not* stop the sun from moving in the heavens at Gibeon because the sun doesn't move at all—the earth moves. Galileo was right; the Bible was wrong.

Biblical believers were not the only ones disturbed by the confusion caused by the new sciences. Philosophers decided that there should be a clear way to establish *the* truth once and for all. They were particularly concerned not to accept any authority, whether the Bible or ancient science. What was needed was a universally accessible method of truth outside of any cultural tradition. No one was more important in this quest for certainty than the French philosopher René Descartes, who has rightly been called "the father of modern philosophy." Modern philosophy has been dominated by Descartes' quest for an intellectual method that can guarantee truth. I have no intention to run through the quarrels of the philosophers about proper method—it is the spirit of the quest for certainty that is important.

Descartes was not just a great philosopher, but also a great mathematician. He invented algebraic geometry, and it was geometry that haunted his search for truth. Descartes, a Catholic, had been educated by the Jesuits in traditional scholastic philosophy. He found it quite unsatisfactory in comparison to mathematics. Philosophers wrangled and never agreed. Mathematicians, in contrast, offered clear, demonstrable truth. Descartes proposed, therefore, to restructure philosophy on a mathematical model. In mathematics one begins with truths that are seemingly unquestionable: "A straight line is the shortest distance between two points." From the basic truths one can deduce any number of subsidiary truths. Not every philosopher then or over the centuries has agreed with the primary truths posited by Descartes' philosophy, but they all wanted to find some rock-bottom truth from which you could either deduce down or build up science. If it wasn't a rational axiom on the top, it might be a simple sense impression at the bottom. The aim was to model science as a construction grounded on an indubitable point of departure.

However one might conceive primary truths, a *foundational model of truth* has been established for natural science and mathematics. The foundational model in one form or another has become *the* method for attaining truth. From the grandest descriptions of the universe to the most everyday occurrence, there is some scientific explanation at hand or to be had. Scientific theory, based as it is on fundamental axioms or observations, goes well beyond common sense perception. We think that the sun moves—it takes special observation and theory to prove otherwise. Atomic theory, gravitational mechanics, genetics, and so on reconstruct everyday perception in terms of processes that can often be reached only by elaborate instrumentation from the first telescope to the latest atomic accelerator. The rise of science has been accompanied, therefore, by the rise of "experts," special observers who know foundational truths from which they derive true conclusions.

I want to emphasize how absolute science can be in determining *the* truth. Although scientists often express skepticism about their theories, in practice science is as severe in excluding "bad science" as any inquisitor hunting down heresy. Whether the Church, with or without infallible popes, can rule definitively on heresy, it is clear that science does. In 1989, two scientists claimed that they had achieved nuclear fusion in a test tube. Nuclear fusion can be achieved under conditions of extreme heat. The hydrogen bomb exploits nuclear fusion, but it takes an atomic fission explosion to achieve the heat necessary to achieve fusion. Fusion in a test tube would be a great advance; it was labeled "cold fusion." The claim was so important that a team of leading physicists was sent to examine the experiments. They were not able to verify the claims. One of the experts was a colleague, and I asked what he made of cold fusion. He called it the "three-miracle theory." If you could get three miracles in a row, events that violated basic laws of physics, you could get cold fusion. Cold fusion is "heretical physics"; it violates the known and certain truths of science.

How does science's foundational model for truth compare with the Church's way of truth? Overall, one could say that there are foundational Christian truths from which we derive the many moral and spiritual instructions of Church. The central truths can seem as far away from common experience as Big Bang cosmology. We say that Church truths are supernatural truths. As in advanced science, there are "experts" (apostles, and their successors like popes and bishops), who, because they possess these truths, proceed to make decisions about doctrine. Astronomers possess the expertise to prove Big Bang cosmology; popes and bishops are experts on the essential dogma and can determine the truths of faith. If someone claims, then, that abortion is in keeping with Christian belief, the experts can examine that claim on the basis of foundational truths and declare truth or falsity.

A foundational view of Church truth analogous to that of scientific foundationalism would explain and fully justify the "authoritarian" cast of the Catholic Church. If Christian truth is modeled on a foundationalist structure like geometry, then there is no disputing the truths of the system. Mathematical truth is not decided by democratic input but by those in the know—mathematicians. The cold fusion case presents a similar pattern for physics. If popes and bishops *know* truths in the sense that mathematicians or physicists know the truths of their fields, the episcopal task is to preserve those truths from falsehood and heresy. The opinions and experiences of the faithful are of no more real relevance to Christian truth than the commonsense experience of the sun moving on the heavens is relevant to the truths of celestial mechanics. Those who want to advance the cause of a "democratic" Catholic Church need to address the fundamental "way of truth" embedded in the claim for authoritative teaching by bishops and popes.

A foundational pattern for Christian truth sounds good—it has certainly been proclaimed many times by leading Church authorities—but there is something seriously askew in a view of Christian truth as analogous to that of science. The most obvious problem is that in Christianity, Jesus is the Truth: "I am the Way, and the Truth, and the Life" (John 14:6). How can a *person* be "the Truth"? I pointed out in the previous chapter, the difference between a teacher of truth and a "savior," the claim made about the resurrected Christ. I want to recapitulate that discussion by turning to the ultimate temptation for Christianity, "the temptation of religion."

The Temptation of Religion: Salvation and Spiritual Wisdom

It obviously sounds absurd to say that a temptation—the last temptation—for Christianity is the temptation of *religion*. I thought that was what the whole thing was about! In suggesting the temptation of religion, I am repeating the observation of the Catholic novelist and philosopher Walker Percy: "Judaism and Christianity are not members in good standing of the world's great religions." Percy's strange comment obviously raises the following question: what is "religion," to which Judaism and Christianity do not belong?

If there is a common notion of "religion," it would probably be something like "a system of *beliefs*." To understand Islam or Buddhism, we ask: What do they believe? On one level that question is easily answered. Islam believes in one supreme God who speaks to Muhammad in the Qu'ran; Buddhists believe in no God at all—or at least, the Buddha thought the existence of God an unanswerable question. Christians believe in the Trinity: three persons in one God. What exactly do these verbal answers accomplish? Not much. One thinks of the oafish Rex in Evelyn Waugh's *Brideshead Revisited*. Rex is taking instruction in the Catholic faith so that he can marry Julia Marchmain. When asked by the kindly priest teaching him Catholic beliefs, "How many persons are there in God?," he answers, "As many as you say, Father." How would we know whether Rex—or anyone—believed in the Trinity as opposed to the supreme God of Islam or the agnostic position of the Buddha? Belief seems to have consequences in action. The theologian George Lindbeck says that when the crusaders cut off the heads of their enemies with the proclamation "Christ is Lord," the statement was false. Muslims no doubt believe that when terrorists blow up innocent people in the name of Allah the all-compassionate, the statement is false. How do I differentiate the genuine actions of Muslims, Buddhists, and Christians along the lines of their stated beliefs? It is because Muslims, Buddhists, and Christians generally are good people that we wonder whether their stated beliefs are all that important. Is religion, then, a matter of catechisms and creeds?

Defining religions in terms of stated beliefs already has a hidden Christian bias, since Christianity seems to have been historically obsessed with creed and dogma. Even Jews are wary of "belief," often differentiating Judaism as "orthopraxy" (right action) from the Christian demand for "orthodoxy" (right belief). Concentration on religious *belief* fits with the notion that religions offer a "philosophy of life," and in some loose sense that is so. When Christianity first came into contact with the ancient world, it was, in fact, regarded as a competitor to various philosophies of life such as Stoicism, Epicureanism, Neo-Platonism, and the like. These are philosophies in the strict sense, general guides for attaining the good life. What Walker Percy is rejecting in his comment is any confusion between Christianity and Judaism and some generic philosophy of life as a set of truths and morals that, if adhered to, will win peace, salvation, or enlightenment.

I am not certain that any of the "world religions" can be properly understood as systems of belief. In one sense they are all into "orthopraxy"—a set of practices, rituals, and meditative techniques that provide "salvation" or "enlightenment." It might be better to look at world religions as one would look at world music. There are major musical practices with elaborately developed traditions of creation and performance. Performers and audiences find the music deeply meaningful and seek every opportunity to participate in the practice. Different musical traditions "mean" different things, but one would hesitate to set down the "philosophy" expressed by an Indian *raga*, or a Mozart symphony. One might offer some verbal metaphor about the sensuous world of the *raga* or the triumphant mood of the *Jupiter* symphony as a suggestion, but only immersion in the practice will reveal the "meaning." To play and participate in these musical works is to live in that special world. The music may uniquely express in nonverbal ways my "belief": "Yes, that is how the world is!" Karl Barth, the great twentieth-century Protestant theologian, said that Mozart's music was "a parable of the kingdom." Barth might even have said that Mozart revealed the "truth" of Christianity more clearly than the thirteen volumes of his *Church Dogmatics*.

Having suggested that religions are best understood by immersion in their practices, one can then begin to differentiate them by those practices. The peculiar "practice" of Judaism and Christianity is centered on a relation to being chosen. Israel is God's chosen people, and Jesus is God's chosen one—through him all humanity is chosen as God's family. The meaning of the religion is read through unique historical actors. "Salvation is through the Jews"; historical Jesus is uniquely Son of God. It is the rootedness in a special history that makes Judaism and Christianity "revealed" religions. According to Rosenzweig, Jews attest their "belief" in the procreation of the Jewish people. Christians attest their belief by worshiping Jesus. Because Jesus affiliates us with God, Christians "procreate" a sacramental family: the Church.

The difference between revealed religion and other strictly religions traditions is particularly clear in the comparison with Buddhism. It is one of the reasons why Buddhism often seems so much more attractive to modern thought. Buddhism is more of a "philosophy of life" because it is not tied to the person of the Sakyamuni. The Buddha is a teacher who offers the Four Noble Truths and the Noble Eight-Fold Path to Enlightenment, but *he* is not the center of the religion. The last thing the Buddha would want is worship of himself similar to the worship that Christians offer to Jesus, or the Jews grant to their special history.

Islam offers a different contrast, particularly to Christianity. Muhammad is not a sage like the Buddha; he is the recipient of special revelation, but his role is sharply differentiated from Jesus in Christian faith. Jesus appears in the Qur'an, where he is revered as a great prophet, but Muslims are deeply offended by Christian claims about Jesus as "god." Jesus is by no means "god"; *lâ ilâha illallâh*, "there is no god but Allah," or, more accurately, "there is no god (deity) but God." The rest of the *shahada*, the fundamental statement of Islam, follows naturally: "and Muhammad is his prophet," or "Muhammad is his messenger." "Qur'an" means "the recitation." To hear the Qur'an chanted is to hear the very voice of God. Muhammad as the one specially commanded to recite is unique among Muslims. One must be specially gifted to recite God's words. Nevertheless, Muhammad recites God's word, but he is not himself God's word, however much he is elevated in and by the recitation. The Christian claim that a human being, Jesus of Nazareth, was in any sense "God-with-us," the "Son of God," is blasphemous to Muslims. "There is no god but God" and "Muhammad is ["only"] his prophet." Islam is not in any way the worship of Muhammad, but Christians *worship* Jesus. In Islam, the uniquely gifted messenger delivers the message; in Christianity the messenger is the message. Jesus himself is the Word of God.

Since this book has concentrated on the *Church*, this sketchy contrast between Christianity and the other world religions explains why a *church* is a necessary part of this faith. The root of a religion-of-Church is the Jewish notion of a "chosen people." In biblical religion one is conscripted into a special community: the chosen family of Abraham, the sacramental family of Jesus. You do not start by believing the story of Creation and following the Commandments—you start from being chosen. You are compelled to right action because that is what being in this chosen family means. Reflection on "being chosen" leads back to Creation and Commandment. Jews are Jews because of what happened in their history with God; Christians are Christians because something has happened to humanity through the life, death, and resurrection of Christ. Jews and Christians may not live up to their status as God's family, but there is no escaping their chosen status, the history within which they are living.

"Chosen" does not mean "superior," a "master race." Traditional Judaism regards itself as chosen, not for its own sake, but for all people. Simeon's proclamation over the infant Jesus presented in the Temple makes this clear for Christianity: "[My] eyes have seen your salvation, which you have prepared in the presence of all peoples, a light for revelation to the Gentiles, and the glory of your people Israel" (Luke 2:30–32). Christians are not to revel in their good fortune as chosen—they are to spread the good news that God has chosen all nations.

One could say that Judaism and Christianity differ from other world religions in the way of taking a journey by following a guidebook, and taking a journey because you trust the guide. The Exodus is the Bible's paradigmatic story. Here is this motley human race wandering in the desert with no clear sense of destination, convinced only that they are lost. Along comes someone, Jesus for Christians, who will lead to where they need to go if they only follow. The people come to trust the guide and, in so doing, stop being wanderers and become a people on pilgrimage. Stranger yet, guide and goal somehow merge. Not only do they trust the guide, they see in the guide a life that conforms to their deepest desire. Pilgrimage people are not just a collection, but also a community defined by a common goal which the guide exemplifies. They are on pilgrimage because they trust and love the guide. The guide, and only the guide, knows the way and *He* is the Way, the one who converts wandering into pilgrimage toward the good life. Early Christianity called itself "the Way" and Vatican II characterized the Church as "the people of God" on pilgrimage. *Church* as a people on the Way is dependent on the guide, and loving the guide who promises to be "with us, all days even to the end of time."

Sketchy as this discussion of Judaism and Christianity and the world religions surely is, it underlines the sense in which these faiths are not, first of all, a set of spiritual truths or divine commands that describe a way to attain salvation. What holds the religion together is not its truths and practical directions, the guidebook to salvation—it is loyalty to the guide, the blessing and terror of being chosen. There is an intense "personalism" in biblical religion because everything depends on relationship to the living guide. The guide speaks to our hearts: "I am the good shepherd, I know my sheep and they know me" (John 10:14). Trusting the guide who knows and loves us changes the dynamics of the human community. This quarrelsome collection of wandering humans has one member who manages to love them all. Imagine a disconnected gang of folks showing up for Christmas dinner. The host loves each and every cranky one assembled. His love changes the inner sense and outward behavior of the normally snarly antagonists. They become a community governed by one who has no enemies—and they can have no enemies in his company.

Jesus does not deliver truths and directives from which we can construct a spiritual guidebook. If that was the story of the Bible, then once we had the guidebook, we could dismiss the guide. *The* truth of Christianity is Jesus, who says *he* is the Truth. Only if he is a living, present reality is there a community on pilgrimage, a Christian Church. Catholicism's centering itself on the "real presence" of Jesus in the sacrament of the Eucharist expresses the reality of Church in a way that catechisms and moral dictates cannot. Despite the canonic writings of the Christian Church, one can say that in a sense revelation is not closed. God remains alive in the ongoing history of the Church; he has not delivered a message and then retreated.

All this no doubt sounds strange, heretical, and downright wrong given common Christian claims that Jesus is a "teacher" who teaches the Beatitudes, the obvious sense in which the Bible is a spiritual "guidebook," and that the statements of the creed are essential to Christianity. Without backtracking on the above view of Christianity, there is, of course, a sense in which the Bible does offer spiritual truths. *The* spiritual truth asserted by Christianity is "Jesus is the Truth": "It is true that Jesus is the Truth; he is the guide, he is the Savior." That is a strange truth to assert, but it implies other truths that make up the content of the creeds. If *Jesus* is the Truth, that implies a special relation to God over and above his human reality. Christians say that Jesus is "Son of God." Deriving truths from the initial unusual claim about Jesus is perfectly acceptable provided one continues to frame these within the personal logic of the Bible: *the* Truth is the messenger with us. The truths, the creeds, any catechism of belief is derived from what we can interpret about the guide, who, in the long run, we finally cannot fit into fixed categories. It is quite appropriate that the resurrected Jesus says to Magdalene, "Do not hold on to me!" The Truth that is Christ alive cannot be confined in the winding sheets of dogma.

Keeping to the claim of the messenger over message has been a special challenge for Christianity because of the temptation of science. If one develops a system of Christian truths, forgetting that all these truths emerge as expressions of trust in Jesus, his life, death, and resurrection, what emerges is a guidebook, not meditation on being guided. It is very easy to confuse "Jesus is the Truth" with "Jesus teaches truths." This tendency is particularly prevalent in Roman Catholicism or, more broadly, "Western Christianity." Why? Christianity grew up within a tradition deeply influenced by Greek philosophy and science—all those rival philosophies of life in the early days. Descartes' scientific foundationalism is a product of that tradition. With the rise of modern science on the foundational model discussed earlier, the temptation arose to adopt a foundational model for Christian truth.

I have already discussed the distortion of Christianity that can occur by patterning the truths of doctrine on something like scientific foundationalism. I noted that all Catholic clergy are instructed in theology. What sort of theology? For many years the theology of the seminaries was cast in the foundational mode. You just had to start with the proper foundational truths derived from reason and scripture. This was the underlying assumption of the "scholastic manuals" that for years provided the textbooks for theological training in seminaries. The scholastic manuals have largely been abandoned, but the spirit of foundationalism lingers. So, while it is true enough that all Catholic clergy have been trained in philosophical theology, the spirit of that theology can be seriously misleading. All too often the theology appears to lay out a guidebook, establishing spiritual truths, but foundationalism is acceptable only if one takes to heart the lesson of the old hymn, "The Church's one foundation is Jesus Christ her Lord." The modern Catholic theologian Hans Urs von Balthasar expresses that spirit when he says that Christians must do theology "on their knees." As the ancient formula states, *Lex orandi, lex credendi* (the law of prayer is the law of belief).

"I Am the Way, and the Truth, and the Life"

I suggested at the beginning of this chapter that a "conservative" Catholic may well regard my three lacks and three temptations as three strengths and three virtues. Put them together and they make up a coherent picture of true Christian faith. Christianity is a system of special supernatural truths revealed by God in the Bible. Central to the revelation is a code of morality that God provides. Teaching and defending biblical morality is a principal task of the Church. Lack of education? Church leaders are properly educated in canon law and dogmatic theology, the objective truths of morality and theology. Lack of listening? The Church is not a democracy; it is a teacher of known truths. Lack of experience? People have all sorts of experiences—what they need are ways to evaluate their experience. Biblical morality and God's natural law set standards for evaluating the wayward experiences of the race.

The conservative picture of Catholicism is not wholly perverse. St. Paul may have said he was "all things to all people" but, whatever he meant by that, it is clear from his admonitory letters that he was no New Age sprite wafting along on the momentary breezes of emotion. He had a message and a gospel. Christians have to heed the message, preach the gospel. The Church is not an empty auditorium rented out to any notion off the street. There is theological learning and special experience. You may need to listen to all sorts of things, but in the long run you need to assess the talk. And so on. The difference between the conservative system and a distorting syndrome rests in how one frames the fundamental message. Paul got it right: "We preach Christ crucified" (1 Corinthians 1:23). Christianity as a system of truths has the virtues of clarity and structure, but Christianity proclaiming Jesus is the Truth personalizes revelation. The modern philosopher Ludwig Wittgenstein put it well: "You can't hear God speak to someone else, you can hear him only if you are addressed.—That is a grammatical remark." The "grammar" of hearing God is that communication must be *cor ad cor* (heart to heart).

Whether in the crispness of canon law or the conclusions of a foundational theology, Catholic leaders and followers often succumb to twin temptations of science and religion as a system of truths. Knowing spiritual truths, religious authority can then speak authoritatively, definitively, and even infallibly. Add to this sense of certainty about Christian truth, the temptation of morality, and you have constructed the thought pattern that has been applied to the abortion issue—not to mention everything else in a presumed Catholic "system" that colors everything from views on homosexuality to the proper English translation of the Roman missal.

Abortion needs to be viewed through the lens of "Jesus is the Truth." Proper Christian assessment of an abortion must arise in a personal interchange—ultimately between Jesus and the woman in her personal story, in the full individuality of her life and circumstance. Archbishop Chaput is half-right when he says that one would have to explain an abortion to Jesus. What seems wrong is that Chaput assumes Jesus will accept no explanation. If Jesus' conduct in the Gospels is a guide, he would not approach abortion as a case study in moral law: "I am the good shepherd, I know my sheep and my sheep know me." Finally, no woman has the same pregnancy or the same abortion story. We are all saints and sinners in our own way.

Does that mean that there are no "objective" standards of morality? Since everyone is individual, are there no universals? Follow that line too far, and one has nothing at all to say about human actions because they utterly elude categorization. As I have argued in several places, that is the wrong conclusion, based on a faulty comparison of scientific objectivity to moral "objectivity." Moral wisdom is akin to artistic judgment. If one is morally wise or has developed artistic sensibility, the rights and wrongs, merits and faults, can be sorted out to arrive at a conclusive judgment. The mistake in understanding moral reasoning is assuming that "objectivity" means that we must *always* agree. Scientists manage to agree because they have structured the game to *only* accept agreement. The prime rule in the science game gets the person, the one with the moral or artistic sensitivity, out of the way because a neutral observer will not color observation by personal factors. But introducing personal sensitivity is precisely what we *must* do to play the moral or artistic game. It certainly is so in the intense personalism of the Christian story. Jesus is no neutral observer—he knows my human heart even better than I.

Jesus says that he is "the Way, the Truth, and the *Life*." I assume he is affirming "life" in the manner of the God of Deuteronomy, a choice not about biological existence, but spiritual life and depth. Paradoxical as it may seem, abortion may be an affirmation of the culture of life. When a woman makes a *deep* choice, often a tragic choice, she may be choosing for life. Even when less than tragic, abortion can be one of the serious but prudent choices that the woman must make in shaping life. Abortion can also be a perversion of the desire for life. Irrational fear, present pleasure, and false values can divert the deep desire for life. The Church should come to abortion as it does to all human actions, saintly and sinful, asking, "Is this a choice for life?"

Afterword

Advice

Abortion is not a topic that seems to conjure much practical wisdom. Passions run so high between pro-life and pro-choice that reflection seems a luxury neither side can afford. Although this is a short book, I am certain it is much too long for partisans. Suggesting that the moral dignity of the fetus may be any less than that of a newborn will persuade the anti-abortionist that there is something wrong in the whole argument. Insisting on the moral seriousness of all abortions alarms the pro-choice folks who fear that moral seriousness will mutate into criminal law. One hesitates to interject any comments into what is largely a dialogue of the deaf, but I will conclude with brief advice to some of the major players.

To Anti-Abortion Advocates

What do you really want to accomplish in your anti-abortion efforts? Do you hope to prohibit abortions by law *or* reduce the number of abortions? If you want to prevent abortions, you will have to recognize that this cannot be done in fact. Even if there were to be a national ban on abortions, abortions would be performed illegally. Are you prepared to accept illegal and dangerous abortions as a fair price for a prohibitory law? Isn't it an exercise in wisdom to seek to reduce the number of abortions and abandon efforts at implausible legal prohibition?

How does the Catholic Church reconcile the claim that abortion at any stage is homicide or murder with the apparent acceptance and even advocacy of laws such as those in South Dakota, which remove all criminal charges from the woman who seeks an abortion? Would it not radically change the tenor and temper of the national debate if you were to admit that the Church does not support the criminalization of women in the case of abortion? As for the abortion provider, can you hold the provider criminally liable for performing an action that a woman has requested, an action for which she bears no criminal penalty?

Reconsidering the political effects of your anti-abortion efforts should have top priority. Not only does it seem that the campaign to legally prohibit abortion is futile, but in concentrating attention on anti-abortion legislation, Catholics have also blunted their capacity to foster significant social programs that are eminently capable of political determination. Nothing will really prevent abortions from taking place, but a simple piece of legislation will ban the death penalty.

While you are considering the political side of anti-abortion, you should also look at the moral argument—particularly the claim that in pregnancy, from conception to birth, we are dealing with an entity with exactly the same moral status. Not only is that a stretch of common moral opinion and common law, it is patently inconsistent with the Catholic Church's own sacramental practice in the matter of miscarriage. Priests do not want to start baptizing embryos in a petri dish.

Finally, in the case of abortion and a variety of other "sins" in the sexual area, it would be a significant advance in moral wisdom to apply the sort of balanced approach that the Church takes on matters of social ethics, where circumstances become essential for deliberation and decision.

To the Politicians

Right-wing, anti-abortion politicians should ponder the lessons above on what is mistaken in the anti-abortion campaign. My principal advice is for so-called pro-choice politicians—which usually means Catholic Democratic officeholders who support *Roe v. Wade*: Stop trying to avoid the issue by saying that you are personally opposed to abortion or that you accept the Church's views on abortion, *but* it is not your responsibility as a legislator to impose your moral will on the country. That is a cop-out. Anti-slavery legislators in the nineteenth century did not retreat into personal opinion or religious cover—they thought that there was something wrong with the law of the land that needed radical change. The problem with abortion for a sensible legislator is not whether it is right or wrong, religious or impious; it is that it cannot be legislated away. When rounded on by one's local bishop for "supporting abortion," don't duck for cover—ask the bishop just what law he would recommend that would accomplish the prohibition of abortion. You won't likely get an answer.

I had the privilege of discussing the problem of criminalizing abortion with the late Senator Ted Kennedy during a visit with the parents of Victoria Reggie, Senator Kennedy's wife. I had been invited by the senior Reggies to meet with the senator because of an article I had published on abortion policy in the Jesuit journal *America*. Senator Kennedy and several other high-level Democrats who joined us were sympathetic to my views about criminalization of abortion. I suggested that a group of the Catholic senators and congressmen seek to meet with the president of the USCCB or a group of the leading bishops to discuss what seemed to me—and they agreed—a fatal flaw in the Church's attack on Catholic legislators who supported *Roe*. When I inquired sometime after whether such a meeting was held and with what results, I was told that the bishops refused to meet. The legislators were told that was a problem between them and their local bishop.

I have come to realize why Catholic legislators do *not* raise the issue of criminalization. If one points out that abortion cannot be punished as Felony 1 murder, it must be because the *moral* claim about abortion is overstated. Challenging the legal position on anti-abortion challenges the moral position. That may be more of a risk than a Catholic politician can bear.

To Pro-Choice

Admit that abortion is not morally neutral. Some abortions are immoral and a permissive culture of abortion is socially undesirable. Women should not want to or be forced to seek abortion as a solution to a problem pregnancy. No one should be "pro-abortion"—it is dangerous in itself, and if it comes to be regarded as just another contraceptive technique, it would have unfortunate social and economic consequences.

Surely you must think that there is more to abortion than just making a choice. People make bad choices all the time and abortion is not excluded from that class. The moral dialogue about abortion is pretty thin: always wrong, always OK. Very few of life's decisions are that clear-cut. As advocates of choice, it would not hurt to admit that there can be bad choices. As advocates of choice, you are best placed to propagandize on wrong choices—like choosing to abort females because males are the favored of the world. Enriching the moral conversation with public statements about good and bad choices would be a real contribution.

To the Courts

Recognize the artifice of *Roe v. Wade*. I had a teacher in graduate school who was famous for a paper titled "The Arbitrary as the

Basis of Rational Morality." Maybe the trimester scheme and the subsequent rulings are the best we can expect, but it also obscures the complex moral story of advancing pregnancy. Eliminating state interest in the first trimester and confining it in the later periods because of the concern about "undue burden" leaves the impression that the moral importance of the fetus has been largely discounted. Mandatory counseling, such as that practiced in Germany, while certainly a burden, does not seem to be an *undue* burden if one wishes to assign moral weight to the final decision. In end-of-life decisions we legitimately seek extensive counsel; beginning-of-life decisions deserve as much. The problem with any amending or qualifying language that would recognize moral status for the fetus throughout is that it is likely to be interpreted too strongly as if the moral status were the same from conception to birth. For *law* there has to be some defining language for the permissible and impermissible, but that line may need to be flexible over time and variable to circumstance.

The Last Word: "Word"

Coming to the end of this effort, I confess that I am very apprehensive about whether it will be of any benefit in the abortion wars that distort our political life. Several months ago I contacted a book agent with the hope that she could locate a publisher. I did not hear and I did not hear. Finally, she contacted me with apologies. She had given the material to an assistant who, after considerable delay, handed it back, saying she had not read it because "she had abortion issues." With that the agent dug into reading it herself. Having worked through the introduction, she expressed qualms because it all seemed so much "semantics." Both these reactions are illuminating and, I fear, predictable. Abortion! Who would want to read another word on the subject! Haven't we had enough! Besides, I have issues [which side?] that would make reading about abortion either repellant or redundant. Then, even if one takes on the text, it is only verbiage, words, "semantics." Pro-life says this, pro-choice says that, and on and on in a battle of slogans. One side's clear reason is the other side's mere rhetoric.

In one sense this is a book about "semantics"; it is about words like "unborn" or "choice" that claim to define the issue but in fact obscure moral complexity. I have tried to heed President Obama's call for "fair-minded words." In that sense, then, the book is about verbiage, words, semantics. Fair-minded words on abortion—or any subject—are created by two factors: accurate attention to the reality of what is discussed, and language that opens discussion rather than closing it down. While I believe that both pro-life and pro-choice advocates fail the test for fair-minded words, most of my concern has been with the coterie of flamboyant Catholic bishops who have seized the public platform. Characterization of abortion as "murder" or "genocide" by these angry clerics is anything but fair-minded. It does not describe the reality—as the legal efforts to ban abortion clearly indicate. Having strayed into unreality, the bishops raise the emotional stakes so that anyone who disagrees seems callous or criminal. Angry exchanges over illusion are not civil discourse. Politics is not a game like professional wrestling.

Concentrating on these loud Catholic voices may seem unfair. Pentecostals are often as flamingly denunciatory as Catholic bishops—and they are likely to wag Bibles at the opposition in the fray. Catholics have a more "rational" approach that suggests a greater possibility for civil discourse. I think that there are serious problems with the reasons advanced by Catholic apologists, but to the extent that they express allegiance to rational argument, they should not reach for a level of certainty that rationality cannot quite attain. Rational argument should invite rational response. Accusing the opponent of promoting killing babies does not lead to rational response.

Are the Catholic bishops interested in a rational response? Rational argument is grounded on rational exchange, but in their polemics, it seems that the bishops slip from the rational to the religious. There is an aura of absoluteness about the anti-abortion position that is a fuzzy amalgam of reason, scriptural citation, teaching of the *magisterium*, and papal infallibility.

It is because the Catholic anti-abortion argument is wrapped in a religious mantle that I have spent so much time on theological topics like Creation and how to read the Bible. It is not only that rational argument demands being open to rational rejoinder—religious discourse has its own problems arriving at absolutes. Religion is grounded in *mystery*, which certainly suggests caution about drawing conclusions. The "mystery" at the heart of religion is not mumbo-jumbo; it is like the mystery of the self. Abortion goes to the core of a woman's sense of self, the mystery of the human heart. Those who would speak about the mystery of God and his care for the human heart should speak with care and compassion, not ready censure and condemnation. Amen.

For Further Reading

Francis J. Beckwith, *Defending Life: A Moral and Legal Case against Abortion Choice* (Cambridge: Cambridge University Press, 2007). (A thoroughgoing, point-for-point defense of the pro-life position.)

Daniel Callahan, *Abortion: Law Choice and Morality* (London: Collier-MacMillan, 1970). (Though outdated in detail, it remains a superb compendium of all the factors that need to be discussed in the abortion debate.)

Stanley Cavell, *The Claim of Reason* (Oxford: Oxford University Press, 1979). (An excellent discussion about why arguments in science, aesthetics, and morality have their own proper rationality and dangers of confusing them.)

Charles E. Curran, *The Catholic Moral Tradition Today: A Synthesis* (Washington, D.C.: Georgetown University Press, 1999). (Though Curran is out of favor with the Vatican, this past president of the Catholic Theological Society of America properly emphasizes the special "stance" that colors moral argument for Christians.)

Charles E. Curran and Richard A. McCormick, S.J. (eds.), *Readings in Moral Theology, No.8: Dialogue About Catholic Sexual Teaching* (New York: Paulist Press, 1993). (Contains some of the classic statements on Catholic sexual morality both officially sanctioned and critiqued by various theologians.)

Daniel A. Dombrowski and Robert J. Delete, *A Brief, Liberal Catholic Defense of Abortion* (Urbana and Chicago: University of Illinois Press, 2000). (As the title indicates, a justification from within the Catholic tradition of abortion under certain conditions.)

Joel Feinberg (ed.), *The Problem of Abortion* (Belmont, Calif.: Wadsworth Publishing Co. Inc., 1973). (An anthology of various articles, including Judith Jarvis Thompson's classic "violinist case.")

John Finnis, *Moral Absolutes: Tradition, Revision and Truth* (Washington, D.C.: Catholic University of America Press, 1991). (A good statement about morality based on "natural goods.")

John T. Noonan Jr., *A Church That Can and Cannot Change* (Notre Dame, Ind.: University of Notre Dame Press, 2005). (A cogent account of how official Church positions have changed on several serious moral issues.)

John Paul II, *Man and Woman He Created Them: A Theology of the Body* (Boston: Pauline Books & Media, 2006). (A very difficult text, not only because of the intricacies of the argument but also due to the fact that it is actually a compilation of talks over some five years and so highly repetitious.)

Jean Porter, *Nature as Reason: A Thomistic Theory of Natural Law* (Grand Rapids, Mich.: Eerdmans, 2005). (A deeply researched discussion of the multiplicity of "natural law" theories and the actual position of Thomistic philosophy.)

Christopher West, *Theology of the Body for Beginners: A Basic Introduction to Pope John Paul II's Sexual Revolution* (Westchester, Pa.: Ascension Press, 2004). (Christopher West is a popular and prolific commentator on theology of the body.)

References

Chapter 1: A Foundational Issue

Statements quoted from the various bishops can be verified though Internet archives of various sources, including the *Boston Globe, New York Times, National Catholic Reporter,* and *The Tablet.* There are also Internet sources for most of the named bishops. There is extensive Internet information about FOCA and its various versions. Official Catholic positions on the range of issues from abortion to euthanasia and stem cell research can be obtained through the website of the United States Conference of Catholic Bishops (USCCB). Information regarding Catholic-Orthodox discussions regarding papal primacy has been reported in *The Tablet.* For an indispensable scholarly account of the conflict of pope and council, see Francis Oakley's *The Conciliarist Tradition: Constitutionalism in the Catholic Church 1300–1870* (Oxford: Oxford University Press, 2003). Oakley argues that those who hold to a uniform tradition of papal autocracy are practicing "the politics of oblivion" by suppressing the claims of conciliarism. Views on abortion in other Christian communions are easily obtained on the Internet. Excerpts from Cardinal Hlond's 1936 pastoral on the Jewish question can also be found on the Internet under his name.

Chapter 2: Abortion and Law

Various legal rulings, state policies, and church documents can be easily obtained via the Internet: *Roe v. Wade, Humanae Vitae,* South Dakota HB 1215 and Initiative 11, and proposed Colorado constitutional Amendment 48. Comments by Bishop Swain of Sioux Falls and the diocese's pamphlet supporting HB 1215 can be obtained from the diocesan website. Daniel Callahan's *Abortion: Law, Choice and Morality* (London: MacMillan, 1979) remains, despite its date, a compendious survey of the legal issues. It is the source for *Rex v. Bourne*. Richard Doerflinger's "Criminal Penalties for Abortion" (*Crisis*, December 1988) and a generous telephone conversation are the basis of my conclusions of where the bishops might stand on the matter of legal penalties. Information for abortion law in other countries is easily obtained by the Internet. NOW, NARAL, and NRA positions can be obtained on their various websites.

Chapter 3: Morality: Not Too Much Theory

The more or less standard natural law theory can be found in various official sources and pronouncements. Paul VI's *Humanae Vitae* is an authoritative source that relies on the biological basis for procreation to derive moral direction. John Finnis and Germaine Grisez are the principal sources for "natural good" theory: John Finnis, *Moral Absolutes: Tradition, Revision and Truth* (Washington, D.C.: Catholic University of America Press, 1991). Jean Porter's *Nature as Reason: A Thomistic Theory of Natural Law* (Grand Rapids, Mich.: Wm. B. Eerdmans, 2005) is an exceptionally careful dissection of natural law theories then and now. For a sophisticated and appropriate philosophic discussion of the nature of moral dialogue, see Stanley Cavell, *The Claim of Reason* (Oxford: Oxford University Press, 1979).

Chapter 4: Rights, Persons, and Pregnancy

Judith Jarvis Thompson's article "A Defense of Abortion" has been widely reprinted (*The Problem of Abortion*, ed. Joel Feinberg [Belmont, Calif.: Wadsworth Publishing, 1973]). For St. Thomas and St. Augustine's views on abortion as murder or not, see Daniel A. Dombrowsky and Robert J. Delete, *A Brief, Liberal Catholic Defense of Abortion*. Julia Kristeva's "*Stabat Mater*" can be found in *The Kristeva Reader*, ed. Toril Moi (New York: Columbia University Press, 1986). A work that argues the pro-choice case from the standpoint of the *persona* of the pregnant woman is Drucilla Cornell's *The Imaginary Domain: Abortion, Pornography and Sexual Harassment* (New York and London: Routledge, 1995). Cornell criticizes the "container" understanding of abortion. On pre-formationist embryology, see Clara Pinto-Correia, *The Ovary of Eve: Egg and Sperm and Preformation* (Chicago: University of Chicago Press, 1997). The controversy over the abortion on the nine-year-old Brazilian girl was widely reported. *The National Catholic Reporter* is a good source on the entire affair from the initial reaction to the ruling by the CDF.

Chapter 5: *Church* Morality

Many of the arguments in this chapter, along with references beyond the text, are contained in my earlier work, George Dennis O'Brien, *Finding the Voice of the Church* (Notre Dame, Ind.: University of Notre Dame Press, 2007). On "stance," see Charles Curran, *The Catholic Moral Tradition Today: A Synthesis* (Washington, D.C.: Georgetown University Press, 1999). Benedict XVI's *Jesus of Nazareth* (San Francisco: Ignatius Press, 2008) is a careful and insightful theological analysis covering the New Testament accounts of Jesus through the Transfiguration. It depends heavily on the Gospel of John and thus on a "high Christology." I reviewed *Jesus of Nazareth* in *The Pope and Jesus of Nazareth: Christ, Scripture and Church*, ed. Adrian Pabst and

Angus Paddison (London: SCM Press, 2009). The chapter is titled "Who's Listening?"

Chapter 6: Notable Lacks and Present Temptations

George Weigel—*Courage to be Catholic: Crisis, Reform and the Future of the Church* (New York: Basic Books, 2002)—is a widely syndicated columnist in conservative Catholic publications and diocesan newspapers. For all intents and purposes, he would be classified as a political "neo-con" with the taste for denigrating opponents that seems to characterize the neo-con style. Data on the popes can be obtained from a variety of sources, such as *The Catholic Encyclopedia*. Information regarding the various bishops was obtained from the Internet. Archbishop Rembert Weakland's autobiography is *A Pilgrim in a Pilgrim Church: Memoirs of a Catholic Archbishop* (Grand Rapids, Mich.: Wm. B. Eerdmans, 2009). Accounts of the history of canon law can be found on the Internet. The "quest for certainty" in modern philosophy from Descartes onward is widely recognized. The "foundational model for truth" has been sharply criticized by a variety of modern philosophers, from pragmatists to analytic philosophers and "existentialists." Walker Percy's view on Judaism and Christianity can be found in *The Message in the Bottle* (New York: Farrar, Strauss & Giroux, 1954). For a succinct account of "mystery" from a Catholic author, see Gabriel Marcel's *The Mystery of Being* (Chicago: Henry Regnery, 1950).

Index

About the Author

George Dennis O'Brien is the former president of the University of Rochester and Bucknell University. He has also been a professor and dean at Princeton University and Middlebury College. He is the author of several books on Catholicism and on higher education, including *Finding the Voice of the Church* and *The Idea of a Catholic University*.